Śrī Soundaryalaharī – an Insight

*

Dr. Ramamurthy N
M.Sc., B.G.L., CAIIB, CCP, DSADP, CISA, PMP, CGBL, Ph.D.

*

*

Name: *Śrī Soundaryalaharī* – an Insight

First Edition: 2021

Author: **Dr. Ramamurthy N,** Chennai.

Copyright ©:   With the author (No part of this book may be reproduced in any manner whatsoever without the written permission from the author).

ISBN (13):   978 93 82237 81 5

Number of pages: 178

Price: ₹ 450.00

Printed at:

Published by:

*****

TABLE OF CONTENTS

Dedication 4

Blessings 5

Introduction 7

Soundaryalaharī 11

Soundaryalahari – *Paramāchāryā* Perspective 14

Soundaryalahari – 100 *Mantras* 27

Soundaryalahari – Verses – Samskrutam 146

Soundaryalahari – Verses – English 164

About the Author 177

Bibliography 180

*****

Dedication

मातृ देवो भव

या देवी सर्वभूतेषु मातृरूपेण संस्थिता ।
नमस्तस्यै नमस्तस्यै नमस्तस्यै नमो नमः ॥

Mātru Devo Bhava

Yā Devī Sarvabhūteṣu Mātru Rūpena Samstitā |

Namastasyai Namastasyai Namastasyai Namo Namaḥ ||

> This book is dedicated with devotion to all the *upasakas* of *Śrī Devī*. There cannot be even an iota of doubt that all will be blessed by *Śrī Ambikai.*
>
> *Dr. Ramamurthy N*

*****

Blessings

Śrī Gurubhyo Namaḥ

Dattatreya Hare Kriṣṇa Unmattānanda Dāyakaḥ
Digambara Mune Bāla Piṣaca Jnāna Sāgarā ॥

Śāntam Dāntam Tapo Niṣṭam Śāntānanda Yatīśvaram ।
Bajāmi Yaminām Śreṣṭam Avadhūtam Aharniśam ॥

The author of this book <u>Dr. Ramamurthy</u> has written many spiritual books and his charity for *Sanatana Dharma* is well known to all.

As such, we are thrilled to learn that Dr. Ramamurthy is publishing this book, on *Soundaryalahari*, which is an important subject for all those who are engaged in Shakta worship.

It is very special that the verses have been provided in English and in Nagara script suitable for recitation and with English translation suitable for understanding and worship. Any verses chant after understanding the meaning, concentration on the God/ Goddess would be easier. In that angle the inner meanings of each verse of Soundaryalahari have been provided in detail. Also, each verse is a *mantra*, which can be chant as *japa* for any particular purpose. Particular *chakra* is attributed to each mantra. All these also have been explained in detail in this book. Therefore, it is a commendable act to publish this book and make *Soundaryalahari* known to all.

I pray to the Almighty Mother that all the devotees understand the supremacy of the author, buy and use this book and become recipients of *Ambal's* grace and that this spiritual work of the author should grow further.

We are very happy to see that Dr. Ramamurthy has compiled and published this book in Tamil also useful for all devotees. We pray to Goddess *Srividya Maha Saubhaghya Parashodashi* daily, for him and his family and for all the loved ones who read this book to get Ambika's blessings and achieve the quadrupedal *purusharthas*.

Let everyone enjoy and live happily.

Happiness   Truth   Auspiciousness

Always in the service of *Sri Devi*.

Jaya Jaya Jagamba – Sri Gurudevadatta

With love

Ayyarmalai   श्रीप्रणवानन्द स्वामिन:
2021   *Srividya Parambika Trust*

 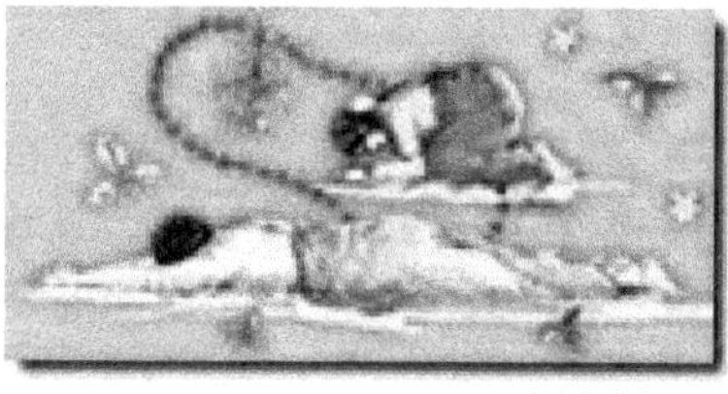

*****

Introduction

ॐ – *Om*

वक्र तुण्ड महाकाय कोटिसूर्य समप्रभ । अविघ्नं कुरु मे देव सर्व कार्येषु सर्वदा ॥

Vakratuṇḍa Mahākāya Koṭisūrya Samaprabha I
Avighnam Kuru Me Deva Sarva Kāryeṣu Sarvadā II

गुरुर्ब्रह्मा गुरुर्विष्णुर्गुरुर्देवो महेश्वरः । गुरुसाक्षात् परं ब्रह्म तस्मै श्रीगुरवे नमः ॥

Gururbrahmā Gururviṣṇurgururdevo Maheśvaraḥ I
Gurusākshāt Param Brahma Tasmai Śrī Gurave Namaḥ II

सदाशिव समारंभां शंकराचार्य मध्यमाम् । अस्मद् आचार्य पर्यन्ताम् वन्दे गुरु परंपराम् ॥

Sadāśiva Samārambhām Śankarācārya Madhyamām I
Asmad Ācārya Paryantām Vande Guru Paramparām II

वागर्थाविव सम्प्रुक्तौ वागर्थप्रतिपत्तये । जगतः पितरौ वन्दे पार्वतीपरमेश्वरौ ॥

Vāgarthāviva Sampruktou Vāgarthapratipattaye I
Jagataḥ Pitarou Vande Pārvatiparameśvarou II

Śrī Ādi Śankara Bhagwat Pādar, the greatest philosopher and thinker, in a short life span of 32 years, has created a collection of art essays Indian culture and the intellectual and emotional integration of this sub continent.

There is one name as "*Śanmada Stāpakar*" in the *ashtotram* of *Adi Shankarar* – the founder of *Shanmada*. He has sub divided our religion of Hinduism, into six sub religion kind of.

Although the worship of these deities had already been existing, Sri Adi Shankarar brought a system into play. These six religions are considered to be the branches of Hinduism. Later, the *Smārtas*, which is not one of the six branches, appear to be a branch of Hinduism, which in some sense is associated with *Shaivam*. In one perspective, they can be called *smārtas* because all the gods are worshipped in the same sense by them – *sama + artha*.

Worshipping of these Gods were there even before *Sri Adi Shankara*. However, he only structured them and hence called as the author of *Shanmada* and Advaita doctrines. He also included one more sub religion called *Koumaaram*. Hence the Advaita concepts are common to all the six sub religions.

Shāktam   Worshipping *Sri Devi* as the primary Goddess. Among the *Shanmadas*, after *Shaivam* and *Vaishnavism*, the most popular god(dess) is *Shakti*. Even the followers of *Shiva*, have a practice of worshipping *Shakti*. *Navaratri* festival is meant for exclusively worshipping *Sri Devi*. *Shakti* worship is practiced and **she** is an important deity who is worshiped all day, irrespective of religion, male, female and caste.

Our mother is the only for this body. After this birth then next birth – another mother. Destruction of the body does not kill *Atma*. There is only one mother for the *Atma*. *Sri Lalita Sahasranama* starts with "*Sri Mātre Namaḥ*". *Ambikai* is the *Jaganmata* – mother of this entire universe. All the energy we have is hers.

Continuously, the fragments of her energy are exhibited to all living organisms. Whatever we do, it is all hers. We cannot do anything. It is wrong to be arrogant thinking that we only did it.

Even if anything is not asked for, **she** will automatically grant them gimmicks, wealth, shine, etc., in the world and then bless them with the bliss also. When we have the supreme Advaita bliss, we become blissful. On the other hand, it is a condition that **she** will settle our *karma* and give liberation one day. Let it be available when it is available. We have a mother who loves us. It is now possible for us to remember her love and pray for her love. Is there anything more to enjoy? The entire world and all living beings will always be happy to think of the dear *Ambika* as a love.

The thought of mother as a goddess, it is turned into – Goddess as mother we worship "*Ambāl Ambikai*". When *Paramātma* form is thought as a mother, more than any other form, the happiness overflows as bliss.

No matter how old are we, we become a baby to mother. We cling to absolute belief and surrender. To obtain the divine nature through the childish nature, we assume the *Paramātma* form into our mother. Hunger or any other desire we cling to the mother as '*amma*' – must hold her strongly.

If we presume *Paramātma* as a *Jagatjanani*, it is not that we enjoy something that does not exist. In fact, *Paramātma*, who is truly in love with all the qualities of the virtues, is the absolute motherhood. The *Paramātma* is everything, hence it blesses us in whatever form, we imagine. In the same way that *Parabrahmam* becomes a mother and with compassion, definitely it comes and satisfies our needs, when we pray, imagining it as a mother.

The practice of worshipping god as a mother is not only in Hinduism but also in Vajrayana Buddhism and in Jainism.

Ādi Shankarar, all over the Bharat that he visited, made everyone feel the pride of *Sri Chakra* and the cult of *Srividya*. Although seemingly he equally treated all the deities, he seems to have given importance to the worship of *Shakti*. He has gracefully authored commentary to *Sri Lalita Trishati* and also given us the noble beings of the *Soundaryalahari*. This is his master piece creation.

Soundaryam means beauty. Mother's beauty and grace are wonderfully transcended in all 100 songs.

One more greatness of the *Soundaryalahari* text is that it is written by *Ādi Shankarar*, an incarnation of Lord *Shiva*. Even if we accept the fact that first 41 verses (*Ānandalahari*) are got from Kailash, it is all the more written by Lord Shiva himself to please Sri Devi Parvati. Can anyone talk about or explain the glory of this text?

According to the 99th verse of Soundaryalahari, those who recite *Soundarya laharī* will know that with the boundless grace of Goddess Parvati, they will also get Saraswathi's blessings.

One can get the grace of the Goddess by chanting Soundaryalahari on Tuesdays and Fridays.

Soundaryalahari is what we recite to worship Ambika and achieve all the comforts. While many books have been published on Soundaryalahari, one may wonder, if there is a need for another book. All the 100 hymns in Soundaryalahari seemingly Devi Stuti – describing Ambal at a glance. Usually, they are recited or sang as songs with music. Each of them is a spell if it is looked inside. There are many philosophies embedded within each. For each spell, there is a *chakra* attached. Each verse is a mantra itself and they can be individually performed as *Japam* for various purposes. This book is an attempt to bring all these out and explain the inner nuances to everyone in a simple way. It is hoped that this will be useful to readers. Everyone who reads this book will get a glimpse of the perfect grace of Sri Devi.

Conventions – Wherever **She** is used to indicate *Śrīdevī* it has been written in bold as **She**. The transliterated Samskrutam or other language words are written in *italics*. When Samskruta words are transliterated in English diacritical marks are used for proper pronunciation like;

ā – as in *R<u>a</u>ma*	*ḍ* – as in mu<u>d</u>
ḍh – as in go<u>dh</u>ood	*ḥ* – visarga in as in *Rāmaḥ*
ī – as in p<u>ee</u>l	*ṇ* – as in pu<u>n</u>
ṛ – as in st<u>re</u>wn	*ś* – as in <u>Sh</u>ankar
ṣ – as in fi<u>sh</u>	*ṭ* – as in cu<u>t</u>
ṭh – as in an<u>th</u>ill	*ū* – as in r<u>oo</u>t

My humble pranams to HH *ŚrīŚrī* **Pranavānanda Swāmijee**, who has blessed me and the readers with his nice introduction and some pleasantries. I am fortunate to have association with people like him. My sincere thanks are due to all who helped me in bringing this book so nicely.

My appreciation and acknowledgements are due to all those who supported in this noble cause.

The readers are requested to feel free in providing comments and feedback to the author. Let all the readers be blessed with glory of Gods.

This book is also being written in Tamil simultaneously

Om Tat Sat

Chennai
2021   **Dr. *Ramamurthy N***

*****

Soundaryalaharī

The *Soundarya Lahari* (सौन्दर्यलहरी) meaning "The waves of Beauty" is a famous literary work in Samskrutam believed to be written by sage *Śrī Ādi Śaṅkarar*.

An anecdotal story. While *Śrī Ādi Śaṅkarar* was on a pilgrimage, he went to the *Kailāś*.

While he was meditating silently there, *Pārvati* and *Parameśwarar* said to each other, "A child has come to our place from below". It looks like we have to give something back to this young boy. "*Śrī Ādi Śaṅkarar* did not know what the two were talking about.

Suddenly *Pārvati Parameśwarar* threw two sets of *olaichuvadis* (palm leaves on which something is written) at *Śrī Ādi Śaṅkarar* from above. Those two touches his both the hands. But he could catch hold of only one of them. The other one was snatched by *Nandi Bhagavan* notwithstanding the fact that they are being taken from Kailash. *Śrī Ādi Śaṅkarar* opened his eyes when he was touched by *Nandi*. There was only a trace in hand. Missing another. When *Śrī Ādi Śaṅkarar* wept and looked up, there *Pārvati Parameśwarar* gave *darshan* to him.

He cried to *Pārvati* – 'Amma' – What *leela* (game) is this? I only got one – Nandi has taken the other. I missed the treasure I found! He cried and lamented.

Then Ambal said, "*Śaṅkara*! Don't cry! Look at me and write from head to toe describing myself. I will show you everywhere. So, don't worry. Be happy with whatever you got".

The first 41 verses were with *Śaṅkarar*. The balance 59 verses remained with *Nandi*.

Śaṅkarar finished composing 59 hymns by his mother's grace, like a free flow flood as his mother ordered him to open up. Thus, *Soundaryalahari* is a collection of 100 songs. This is the story of *Soundaryalahari's* origin.

The first 41 shlokas are called *Ānandalaharī*. It is said that Lord *Shiva* composed these verses and made *Pārvatī* happy. The other 59 shlokas are called *Soundaryalaharī*. However, colloquially, entire 100 verses have started to be called as *Soundaryalaharī*.

Some believe the first part "Ananda Lahari" was etched on mount Meru by Ganesha himself (or by Pushpadanta or by Lord Shiva). Sage Gaudapada, the teacher of Shankara's teacher Govinda Bhagavadpada, memorised the writings of Pushpadanta which was carried down to *Śrī Ādi Śaṅkarar*. Its hundred and three shlokas (verses) eulogize the beauty, grace and munificence of Goddess Parvati/ Dakshayani, consort of Lord Shiva.

Soundarya Lahari was composed in Kashmir. The Soundarya Lahari is not only the collection of holy hymns, but also a tantra textbook, giving instructions Puja on Sri *Yantra* and worshiping methods, 100 different hymns, 100 different *Yantra*s, almost one to each shloka – describes the appropriate tantra method of performing devotion connected to each specific shloka and details the results ensuring therefrom. There are many interpretations and commentaries but best of these are arguably those that provide word to word translations, as also the *Yantra*, the devotion to be performed and the results of the devotion.

Verses 1 41 describe the mystical experience of the union of Shiva and Shakti and related phenomena. In fact, it opens with the assertion that Only when Shiva is united with Shakti does he have the power to create. Verses 42 100 are more straightforward; they describe the physical beauty of the Goddess and are sometimes referred to as the Soundarya Lahari itself.

The Soundarya Lahari is not only a poetic text. It is a tantra textbook, giving instructions on Puja and offerings, many *Yantra*, almost one to each shloka; describing the tantra technique of performing devotion connected to each specific shloka and details the results ensuing therefrom. There are many interpretations and commentaries but best of these are arguably those that provide word to word translations, as also the *Yantra*, the devotion to be performed and the results of the devotion.

Many scholars, however, refer to the entire text with one name, namely, Soundarya Lahari.

First 41 verses cover the detailed account of internal worship of the Mother. It consists of systematic exposition of the concept of kundalini, Sri Chakra, mantra (verses 32, 33). This depicts the Supreme Reality as non dual but with a distinction between Shiva and Shakti, the power holder and Power, Being and Will. The Power, that is, the Mother or Maha Tripura Sundari, becomes the dominant factor and the power holder or Shiva becomes a substratum. The first verse itself clearly describes this idea. "United with Shakti, Shiva is endowed with power to create; or otherwise, he is incapable of even a movement." The same idea is brought out in verse 24, "Brahma creates the universe, Vishnu sustains, Rudra destroys, and Maheshwar absorbs everything and assimilates into Sadashiva. On receiving mandate from thy creeper like brows, Sadasiva restores everything into activity as in the previous cycle". Such prominence of the Mother can be seen in verses 34 and 35 also.

There are several legends about this work. Verses 1   41 are the original work of Lord Shiva, shedding great light on the ancient rituals of Tantra, *Yantra* and various powerful Mantra. The remaining verses, that is, 42 100 are composed by *Śrī Ādi Śaṅkarar* himself, who is believed to be an incarnation of Lord Shiva, which mainly focuses on the appearance of the Goddess. Yet another legend says that once when *Śrī Ādi Śaṅkarar* was visiting Kailash, Lord Shiva was writing about the beauty of Goddess Parvati on the walls of their home. Shiva rubbed what he wrote as he didn't want *Śrī Ādi Śaṅkarar* who was an outsider reading about the beauty of his wife. But *Śrī Ādi Śaṅkarar* had seen some part of the writings and with his superior mind recollected the rest. Thus, he composed the Soundarya Lahari (waves of beauty of the Devi).

There are more than 36 commentaries on the Soundarya Lahari in Sanskrit itself. Among the better known are commentaries by Lakshmidhara, Kameshvara Soori (viz. Arunamodini), Kaivalyashrama (viz. Sowbagyavardhini) and Dindima.

Soundarya Lahari was translated into Tamil in the 12th century by Virai Kaviraja Pandithar. He titled the book Abhirami Paadal. W. Norman Brown translated it to English which was published as volume 43 of the Harvard Oriental Series in 1958. There are many other English translations with commentaries on Soundarya Lahari done by various authors.

Let us immerse ourselves in this immortal treasure of nectar upto some extent possible.

*****

Soundaryalahari – Paramāchārya Perspective

The very words of *Paramāchāryā* (from the book *Deivathin Kural* – Voice of God) – The beginning of *Soundaryalaharee* Verse 23 – *tvayā hrutvā* brands *ambā* as a thief! You have already appropriated half of His body. And you were not satisfied. Now You have appropriated the other half also. The gymnastics of words is delightful. In the word *aparitruptena* there is an *apari*. This is in the first line. In the second line there is *aparam*. The latter word means other. But *apari* is the opposite of *pari*. *Pari truptena* means; by one who is fully satisfied. The *pari* stands for 'fully'. Hence *apari truptena* means; by one who is not satisfied fully. Having taken only half the body how can **She** have a full satisfaction? **She** had only a partial satisfaction! That is what is indicated by the *apari truptena*. It is the left side of the Lord's body that belongs to *ambā*. This is the age old tradition. That is how *Ādi Shankarā* expected to see *ambā* when he sought **Her** *darshan*. But what did he see? He expected to have a darshan of Father and Mother in the *ardha nāreeshvara* form. But what he saw was the Mother's form, including the right side. Father is crystal white and Mother is crimson red. But what he saw was *Sakalam Arunābham* – fully crimson red. He expected to see a masculine form on the right side, but what he saw was *Kuchābhyām Ānamram*. Hence the *Āchārya* concludes – in poetic fancy, of course – that the other (right) half of *Shiva's* masculine body also has been taken over by *ambā*. It may be noted that Lord *Shiva* himself is described in the *Vedas* as *taskarānām patiḥ* the head of all the thiefs! But *Ambā* has executed a theft on Himself, by stealing the other remaining half of His body though **She** had been, with great condescension, given half of His body (the left side) already! And it is delightfully interesting to note that the poet in the *Āchārya* does not say that the other half of the body has also been captured. He dares not, even in poetic fancy, make that charge assertively against *Ambā*. He only says *shangke* – I suspect. When one says "I suspect" one should give reasons. He has given two reasons. Wholly crimson red is one; the features of the chest is another. But this is not enough. To support his charge further, he gives two more, which clinches the issue. These are the two features – *Trinayanam* (three eyes) and *Kutila Shashichoodāla Makutam* (crown that includes the half Moon in it). These two are exclusively the features of Lord *Shiva*. His name, even according to the Vedas is *Tryambaka*. In the preliminary *mantras* to the *Rudraprashna*, the meditation verse beginning with *Āpātāla nabhasthalāntha....* the second line describes Him as *Jyoti Sphātika Linga Mouli Vilasatpoornendu...* which means that as the *Shiva linga*, He has the full Moon on His top. When the same *Devata* is figured anthropomorphically as a Person, He would have on His head, only a half Moon. Thus, the three eyes and the crescent Moon belong to the Lord. But when the *Āchārya* had the *darshan* he saw both these in *ambā* Herself!

In fact, the *darshan* he had was of *Kāmeshvaree*, the goddess of *Soundaryalaharee*. *Kāmeshvaree* has a third eye in **Her** forehead. In the meditation verses of *Lalitā sahasranāma*, the verse begins with *sindhoora aruna vigrahām*. The *sindhoora* colour ascribed to the form here is the crimson red colour, indicated by *Sakalam Arunābha* in this current *verse*. Following that, the meditation verse goes on next to *trinayanām* (three eyed). Thus, the red colour and the three eyes are natural to the form of *Kāmeshvaree*. But in the present verse the *Āchārya* takes the stance, in his poetry, that the former (namely, the red colour) is naturally **Hers**, whereas the latter (namely, the three eyes) has been appropriated from the Lord's form!

Continuing the meditation verse, we have the expression *Tārānāyaka Shekharām* meaning, who has the Moon on **Her** head. This the Acharya has used in his verses as *Kutila Shashi Choodāla Makutām*. Thus, the *Āchārya* has made a *nindā stuti* (praise by pointing out faults) of *ambā* by using the same four characteristics which *ambā* has, according to the meditation verses, namely, red colour, three eyes, crescent Moon on the head and the feminine form. But two of them he says *ambā* has appropriated from the Lord. In fact, it is the *Āchārya* who has appropriated two of the four all of which rightfully belong to **Her**, by accusing **Her** of appropriating those two from Her Lord.

It is not that the *Āchārya* did not know. He certainly would know that all four are natural characteristics of *Lalitāmbā*   *trinayanā* (the three eyed) is one of **Her** names occurring in the *Lalitā Sahasranāma*. *Chāruchandra kalādharā* is also another. In *Shymalā Dandaka* of *Kalidasa*, we have him addressing **Her** as *Chandra Kalāvatamse*. (**She** who has ornamented **Her** head with the Crescent Moon). Thus, *Ambā* does have these two characteristics as **Her** own. In images of olden times, I have myself seen **Her** being depicted thus. But the ordinary common folk still think that the concepts of three eyes and the crescent Moon on the head are exclusively those of Lord *Shiva*. And, the *Āchārya*, in his poetic excitement, joins the common folk and creates a *Nindāstuti*!

There is still another angle. The verse under discussion revels in the idea of *Ambā* having appropriated the Lord's characteristics and also his right half. But the poetic world knows that it is the other way round. It is the Lord who has appropriated **Her** characteristics and legitimately what is due to Her!

In the *Ardha Nāreeshvara* form the third eye is common to both the masculine and the feminine forms. It is by the third eye He consumed Cupid, the God of Love, to ashes. Hence the credit of that consumption should go half each to the Lord and *Ambā*. But who is known as *Kama Dahana Moorti*? It is He. Similarly, when *Kāla*, the God of death, was attempting to get the *Markandeya*, an ardent devotee of Lord Shiva, into his death noose, he was vanquished by the left leg of the Lord, and thus He has earned the name *Kala Samhāra Moorti* and known as such as the world over. But the left leg in the *Ardha Nāreeshvara* form actually belongs to *ambā* and hence the credit for vanquishing *Kāla* should wholly go to *Ambā*. Thus, on both counts it is Her that should be faulted for appropriation and not **She**!

Well, we could go on like this. But the final essence of all this discussion is that there is no appropriation on either side. It is all one form and one Supreme. The Lord form is totally in **Her** and Her form is totally in His. *Lalitā* **Herself** is *Shivashaktyaikyaroopinee* (999th name); this *advaita* (non duality) is the bottom line of the whole thing.

In another verse # 54, the three colours white, red and black which stand for *satva*, *rajas* and *tamas* are presented from a different perspective. The river Ganga is white. It comes from Shiva's matted hair.

Yamuna river is black, because it has an inseparable relationship with Lord Krishna. The third one is *Sarasvati*, which is invisible but flows under Ganga and Yamuna as an underground current. Instead of *Sarasvati*, the *Āchārya* takes the Sone river, which is red. The meaning of *Sona* is red. If Ganga is taken as *Shiva* and Yamuna is taken as *Vishnu*, then the Sona is to be taken as *Ambāl*.

There is a lot of beauty implicit in *Soundaryalaharee*. One of these is the mention of 'Meenakshi'. This also concerns the 'eye'. 'Meenakshi' itself means the 'fish eyed'. **Her** very fame from ancient times has always been centered upon the beauty of **her** eyes. Of such a great *Devee*, apparently neither of the two great works on *Devee* has spoken. These two are Lalitā *Sahasranāma* and *Soundaryalaharee*. But this is only a first impression. If we carefully look into these works, we would come to know there is no necessity to default them for this.

For, though there is no explicit mention, *Meenakshi* is implicitly mentioned in *Lalitā Sahasranāma*. In fact, it is this very implicitness that adds a greater importance to that. *"Vaktra lakshmee pareevāha chalan meenābha locanā"* (18th name) is one of the names in the *Sahasranāma*. *'vaktra lakshmee'* means the brilliance of *Ambāl's* face. It is like a great flood (*pareevāha*). When the dalliance of the face runs as a flood of water, there ought to be fish in that flood! Where are the fishes? The long eyes of *Ambā* are the fishes. *'locana'* means 'eye'. (*'lokana'* means 'sight' or 'glance'. By the very fact that it is 'seen', the world is called *'loka'*). The *'locana'* that resembles 'a fish' generates the word *'meenābha locanam'*. Instead of saying *'Meenakshi'* explicitly, it is mentioned as *'Minābha locanā'*. Well, that takes care of one 'default'!

In *Soundaryalaharee*, where the verse # 49 talked about the relationship of **Her** eyes to various cities, *'Madhura'* occurs. Hence by giving the name of the city of *Meenakshi*, we may take it *Meenakshi* has been mentioned. In addition to this there is verse # 56. The first two lines of 56th verse is;

Tavāparne karne japa nayana paishunya chakitāḥ I
Nillyante toye niyatam animeshāḥ shapharikāḥ II

Tavāparne has to be broken as *tava aparne*. *Aparnā* is the name of *Ambā*. The name *Aparna* means '**She** who did not even eat the leaves. In her manifestation as the daughter of the Mountain King, when **She** was doing penance in order to be wedded to Lord Shiva, **she** adopted such a terrific self discipline, wherein, **she** did not even have the fallen leaves as **Her** food.

Japa nayana paishunya chakitāḥ (talking – eyes – tell tale – trembling) trembling in fear that **your** eyes (that extend up to the ear) are perhaps carrying tales of slander (about them) *tava karneḥ* to **your** ears.

Why do fish never swim in the upper regions of the ocean and instead always stay in deep waters? The *Āchārya* here imagines an interesting reason. He sees *Ambāl's* eyes which extend up to **Her** ears. **She** is always rolling Her eyes on all sides in order that not a single being in the universe misses **Her** blessed glance of protection. And hence they now and then reach the extremities of the eye and appear as if they are touching the ears! And the fishes think – that is when the eyes say something secretive into the divine ears. They think defensively that the

Devee's eyes are perhaps telling tales about them (the fishes); because they always think that the fish eyed looks of the *Devee* are only competing with them as rivals in terms of fast movements. And naturally they are afraid, the *Devee* might take it on them and therefore they stay in deep water! They know that if they are really put to test, they will lose in competition with *Ambāl's* eyes both in the beauty as well as in fast movement.

In the *Meenakshi* temple at Madurai, there is a tank called 'The tank of the Golden Lotus'. There are no fishes in that tank. The folklore is that they don't come there because they know they cannot compete with the beauty of the eyes of Goddess *Meenakshi*. Thus, the *Āchārya* in making a comparison of *Ambāl's* eyes with fishes and in painting a picture for us of the fishes not wanting to show up before **Her**, has really subtly hinted to us of Goddess *Meenakshi* in this verse!

"How could *Śrī Ādi Śankarar*, who preached the *jnana marga*, have promoted this work (*Soundaryalahari*) of *bhakti*? It cannot be his", say some who profess 'Philosophy'. But our *Acharya* was not a professor who isolated philosophy as a separate discipline. Having written very profoundly on *advaita* and its deepest implications in his several *Bhashyas* and the other works of his, he promoted the spiritual pursuit of the common man by writing and talking about the need to follow one's *swadharma* by *Karma* and *Bhakti*. His intent was to raise the common man from his own level. For this purpose, he went from one pilgrim center to another all his life and composed hymns after hymns and also established *yantras* in temples.

The philosophers argue – Jnani says everything is One. But *Bhakti* can happen only when there is the duality of the devotee and the deity. Therefore, they say, the jnani can never be a *bhakta*. These philosophers cannot themselves claim to have the Enlightenment of *advaita*! But there have been those who could have so claimed, like the sage *Suka, Madhusudana Saraswathi* or *Sadasiva brahmam*. If we carefully study their lives, we will know that they were devotees of God in the fullest sense of the word and have themselves written works of *Bhakti*. Even in our own times *Ramakrishna Paramahamsa* has been a great devotee of Mother Goddess and *Ramana Maharishi* has done works of devotion on God *Arunachaleshvara*. Again, on the other side, great devotees like *Manikka vasagar, Nammazhvar, Arunagirinathar, Tayumanavar* and all have themselves been convinced *advaitins* and this is reflected in innumerable flashes in their compositions.

If a *jnani* should not do a *Bhakti* composition, then I would say that he should not also do a work of *jnana*. Why am I saying this? Let us go back to the definition of a *jnani*. "The world is all *maya*; the thinking of people as if they were separate *jeevatmas* is nothing but Ignorance" – with such a conviction through personal experience, they have thrown away that Ignorance as well as its basic locus, the mind and they live in the non dualistic state of "'I' am everything" – such should be the status of the *jnani*; shouldn't it be so? Such a person preaching, or writing a book, even if it be about the subject of *jnanam* – is it not a contradiction? Unless such a person thinks there, is a world outside of him and there are *jeevatmas* outside, how can he think of 'teaching'? Teaching whom? And when we look at it this way, all those great teachers of *jnana* should really not be *jnanis*! What power will there be for such a teaching about *jnana* from teachers who are not *jnanis* themselves?

On the other hand, what do we observe in our experience? Whether it is the teaching about *jnana* in the Gita, or the Viveka *Choodamani* of our Acharya, or the *Avadhoota Gita* of *Sri Dattatreya* or the teaching in the *Yoga Vashishta*, or a song of *Tayumanavar* – even when we just read these, we feel we are being taken beyond the curtain created by *maya* to some distant peaceful state of Calm. Just by reading, in one's spiritually ripe stage, such teachings, there have been people who have renounced the world and reached the state of Bliss in one Self!. If these teachings had not been written from that spiritual apex of Experiential Excellence, how could such things have ever happened?

Therefore, however much by your intellectual logic, you argue whether a *jnani* can get *bhakti*, how the jnani can do any preaching and so such possibilities cannot exist and so on, these are certainly happening, by the Will of the Lord which is beyond the Possible and the Impossible.

It is only the Play of the Lord that the *jnani*, who is non dualistic internally, appears to do things in the dualistic world. His mind may have vanished, *maya* might have been transcended by him; but that does not mean that the outside world of *jeevatmas* has disintegrated. What do we gather from this? There is a Super Mind which does all this and in some mysterious way is compering and directing the entire universe. And it also means that it is the same Supra Mind that is making the minds of men revolve in the illusion of *maya*. It is that Power which is known in advaita scriptures as *saguna brahmam* or *Ishvara*. In the scriptures devoted to shakti or Shiva, whenever they call the Actionless *nirguna brahmam* as 'Shivam' they call this *saguna brahmam* as 'Shakti', 'Para *shakti*' or 'Ambal'. Just as that *nirguna brahmam* exhibits itself and acts as the *saguna brahmam*, so also, it must be presumed, that the enlightened *jnani* also does his external actions and that again, is the work of the *Saguna Brahmam*!

What is the path of *jnana*? It is the effort through self enquiry and meditation for the eradication of the mind and vanquishing of *maya*. But the other path is to dedicate oneself and all one's thoughts and actions to that very *Para shakti* (who produced this *maya* on us) with an attitude of devotion. It is like giving the house key to the thief himself! However much the *Para shakti* may play with you and toss you and your mind hither and thither, her infinite compassion cannot be negated. Only when we separate and rejoin, we realise the value of that union. To pray to Her for that reunion and for Her to get us back to Her in answer to our prayers – this is the great Leela of Duality wherein She exhibits Her Infinite Compassion! Hence when one prays with *Bhakti* for such release, she releases Him by giving Him that Wisdom of Enlightenment.

It is wrong to think that the goal of *Bhakti* lies in the dualistic attitude of being separate from God. It is by this wrong assumption that people ask the question – How can a *jnani* exhibit *Bhakti*? In the very path of *Bhakti* wherein it appears there is an embedded duality, the same *Bhakti* would lead the practitioner to the stage where he will ask – Oh God! May I be one with You! This is the subtle point which the questioning people miss. When that stage comes to the devotee, the very *Para shakti* known as *karya* brahmam or *saguna brahmam* will bless him with that *jnana* that takes him to the non dual karana *brahmam* or nirguna *brahmam*.

Not everybody can practice the path of *jnana* that brings the realisation of the *maha vakyas* by *Shravana* (hearing), *manana* (thinking and recalling) and *nididhyasana* (contemplating). Only when the mind vanishes one can realise the Self as the Absolute *brahmam*. If that is so, the real question is – How to kill the truant mind, which refuses to be subdued, much less vanquished? The very effort of vanquishing the mind has to be done by the mind only. How can it kill itself? The palm can slap another; but it cannot slap itself. Though we are thus brought to a dilemma, there is a supreme power which has created all these minds. So instead of self effort to kill our minds, we should leave it to the *Para shakti* and surrender to Her. Instead of falling at the feet of the witness for the prosecution we fall at the feet of the prosecutor himself! Then She will help us quell the mind; She will grace us with the necessary *jnana*.

Either She might totally eradicate your mind and give you the peaceful state of "I am shiva" (*shivoham*) or She might tell you from within

"Look, after all, all this is My Play. The Play appears real to you because of *maya*. I shall totally erase that *maya* view for you. Then you can also be like me, with that calm non dual bliss inside and having on the outside a mind which is untouched by *maya*. Thereby you can also be a witness to all this worldly Dance. You will thus see yourself in Me and see Me in all the worldly multiplicities. In other words, instead of making the mind non existent, your mind will then be full of Me"

And She might make you just exactly that way. But I know your worry. You constantly worry about the impossibility of transcending *maya*, of eradicating this worldly vision and of vanquishing the mind. You keep worrying to the extent of almost weeping over it. To such a willing seeker She replies –

"Why do you worry and weep like this? You are worrying that you cannot discard the world from your view. But you forget that the world was not you're making. This Sun and Moon, mountains, trees, oceans, animal kingdom, and the millions of living beings and categories – all this was not created by you.

"When that is so, you are worrying about the little 'you' that you are, and you forget that this little 'you' also was not your creation. Instead of thinking all this is not only one but one with Me, your *maya* clouded view makes you think they are all different and distinct. And even that *maya* view that clouds you, again were not your making!

"My dear child, you are caught up in the web of the world, a mind and a *maya* cloud – all this is My making. Did I not make Krishna say to you – *Mama maya duratyaya*? (My *maya* is intranscendable). I have also told you there that it is made by the Power of God. If you had made it all, then you could have overcome them. But it was all made by Me in the fullness of Power.

"You *jeevas* have only little fragments of that Power. So, if you cannot eradicate the world, the mind and the *maya* that I have made, you don't have to cry over it. It is not in your Power. It has to take place only by My Grace. Come nearer to Me through Devotion! I shall do the eradication in proper doses for you.

"That somebody is able to control his mind and is able to walk on the path of *jnana* – that again is My own Grace. It is I who have granted that privilege to him. What appears as many and different must be seen as one. To crave for that view is what is called *"advaita vasana"*. One gets it only by My Grace".

Now the Paramacharya, who has been talking in the words of the Mother Goddess, continues on his own.

There is another novelty here. Even the *jnani* who has had the non dual Enlightenment, still enjoys the play of *maya*. He sees the different things; but knows they are all one. Just as a spectator of a play who is not playing any role in it, the *jnani* enjoys the playful novelties of *maya* and revels in his devotion to that Para Sakthi who is the author of it all. To be keeping such jnanis in this dual non dual state is also the work of Mother Goddess. Mark it. It is not that the *jnani* is showing Devotion just for the sake of others only. No, by himself he is indeed thinking

"What a pleasure to witness this dualistic play of the non dualistic One! What a multiplicity of beauty, panoramic variety and continuity of Love!" Thus, reveling in that blissful vision, he continues to pour out his own love (*bhakti*) to that Transcendental Power from the bottom of his heart. This tribute to the *jnani* has been given by the great Teacher *Suka* himself.

Shrimad Bhagavatam (1 7 10) says –
> *Atmaramashca Munayah Nirgrantha Apy Urukrame*
> *Kurvanty Ahaitukim Bhaktim Itham Bhuta Guno Hariḥ* l

– Those who revel in the Self, even though rid of all attachments, show a causeless bhakti towards the Lord, just naturally.
On the one hand the devotee who has yet to get the Enlightenment enjoys the devotional state for the very reason of getting the Enlightenment; on the other hand, the one who is already enlightened and is a *jeevan mukta* shows his *bhakti* for the sake of enjoyment of that bhakti and not for any other reward or purpose.

Paramacharya continues to speak the words of the Goddess – "Thus I am the One who gives this new Bhakti in the state of *jnana*. And I will be the One who will give you that *jnana* to you, my devotee, when the time is ripe. Don't you worry. You have come to Me as your Mother. I will take care of you. The bondage in which I threw you shall be removed from you by Myself. You need not have to keep on crying for 'Release'. Once you know I am the only One there is, hold on to that steadfastly; there is no question of 'Release' thereafter. 'Release' from what?

"Let jnanis think that they will get the Ultimate Peace only when the duality awareness goes away from them and let them go their own way of Enquiry of the

Self. When you feel you don't have the interest or the stamina to go that way, don't feel bad or incomplete. Come through the path of Love. See the multiplicities. But instead of seeing them as different and separate, try not to forget that the basis of all of them is the single Me. Love Me from your heart and view everything through Love. Encompass everything in Love. I shall raise you to the Ultimate Enlightenment by My Love and Grace".

Thus, arises the godly experience that is blessed by the Mother Goddess. By Mother Goddess I also mean the Lord God, the *paramatma*, and also the individual favourite deity of each of us. It is the same supreme Power that engulfs you into the *maya*, that graces you as *saguna brahmam* and also takes you to that blissful state of *jnana*.

Finally let me also say this. By the very fact that the *jnani* writes a book on *jnana*, it must follow that he should also write on Bhakti. For, writing a book means communicating with others. So that means he has accepted the presence of a world of duality in which he has to communicate and educate. The *jnani* as he is, must have already 'descended' to this world of duality and   decided to raise the commonfolk to his level. He who knows that the source of all this duality is that Infinite Compassionate God–principle, would ipso facto have no compunctions for making a hymn of praise for that Ultimate in its *saguna* form. And he also knows that it is that very same Power that prods him on to make this hymn. So where is the contradiction here?

 But if you contend that he is writing *jnana* works for the benefit of the world – '*loka sangrahartham*' without any '*kartrutva buddhi*' – the awareness of doer ship – then with the same non awareness of doer ship he can write both *jnana* works and bhakti works. What and where is the difference? The World welfare (*loka kalyanam*) is the purpose. It is the Lord who is affecting the welfare through the hands and mouth of these chosen *jnani*s. And the most efficient way for the *jnani*, the Lord knows, to reach the masses, is to propagate hymns of praise of the divine, pilgrimage to holy centers, installation of mystic *Yantra*s, and all the way down to ritual worship.

There are three superlative hymns of praise on Mother Goddess in the form of Lalita. Chronologically they are; '*Arya dvishati*' (also called '*Lalita stava ratnam*') a 200 shloka piece by Sage Doorvasa; 'Soundaryalahari' which is actually made up of two parts – 'Anandalahari', a 41 sloka piece brought from *Kailash* by Adi Sankara and 'Soundaryalahari' the 59 shloka piece composed by *Śrī Ādi Śaṅkarar* himself, the two pieces together going by the popular name of *Soundaryalahari* by *Śrī Ādi Śaṅkarar* and '*Panca shati*' (a 500 *shloka* piece) by the poet Mooka.

Durvasa's Arya *dvishati* gives us a spiritual experience of the presence of the Almighty Goddess in the very words of *Arya dvishati*. In this he describes the complicated structure of the Sri chakra. The Goddess's Grace descends on those who read and recite such hymns of praise composed by great devotees who have already merited the descent of Her Grace on them. *Durvasa, Śrī Ādi Śaṅkarar* and *Mooka* are three such. Such Grace exhibits itself first in the eloquence of these hymns. And the result is, the devotee who revels in the recitation and repetition of these hymns, himself gets that eloquence and flow of language and of speech. The Goddess gave such an eloquence to *Mooka*. '*Mooka*' means dumb. We do not know what name he had before. But from the moment he composed the five hundred slokas in Her praise, we have known him as the poet *Mooka*! Both the *Arya dvishati* and the *Mooka pancashati* bring to our vision the majestic splendour of the form of Mother Goddess like an expert painter's masterly painting. The third one, the Soundarya lahari is the crowning glory of all three and of all hymns of praise of the Mother Supreme.

Of *Soundaryalahari* it may be said that there never was one like it, nor ever will be. It has a perennial charm that does not satiate. And its majestic eloquence is unbeatable. In his bhaja govindam our Acharya uses very elementary words because it happens to be the alphabet of Vedanta. But here he is describing the indescribable. So, he uses words very precisely. Consequently, the vocabulary turns out to be difficult. But the words chosen only add to the lilting charm of the poetry that he weaves. The meter used is 'shikarinee', meaning "that which is at the apex". It has 17 syllables for each of the four lines.

Through the descriptions of the Goddess's form that make up the latter 59 slokas, he brings *Ambaal* right before our mental eyes in all Her majesty, grace and splendour and overwhelms us by the bliss which the very words and metaphors pour on us. Just as a master sculptor dedicates each movement of his chisel to the object of his sculpture, he transforms each word, as it were, by his own spiritual experience of the Goddess and thus in turn we readers feel the words themselves constitute the Goddess.

It is not only blissful poetry, but blessed poetry. Such blessedness arises not because of any flowery language, but by the fact the Acharya is himself blessed! 'Mother, this hymn is nothing but a composition of yours in your own words' ("*Tvadiyabhir Vagbhiḥ Tava Janani Vacam Stutir Iyam*" – Verse no. 100), says he in the concluding line. Inspirations of great saints and sages, not only benefit mankind by their inspired poetry, but bring to successive generations, an inspired contact with the great men, even long after they have passed away. Thus, our Acharya in enabling us to have a *'darshan'* of the Goddess herself, gives us, in addition, a *'darshan'* of himself!

The concept of 'intense' devotion does not care for the language used, or for the manner of worship. It is the intensity of devotion and depth of feeling that matter. But getting that intensity and depth is the most difficult thing. That is exactly what eludes us. Now that is where the beauty of such blessed poetry like *'Soundaryalahari'* excels. Whether you understand it or not, whether you pronounce the words correctly or not, the very attempt itself of reciting it produces in you the needed bhakti! This is the word power of the words of such blessed poetry. The vibrations of the words give us all the material and spiritual success. We have only to keep the objective of bhakti steadfast in our minds. Everything else just follows.

Of all the *stotras* that our Acharya has done, it is the Soundaryalahari that is the topmost. The *Ashtottara Namavali* of the Acharya has a name *"Soundarya Lahari Mukhya Bahu Stotra Vidhayakaya Namah"* meaning – "prostrations to the one who composed many stotras with *Soundaryalahari* as the prime one". Of the *Bhashyas* that he wrote, 'Brahma Sootra Bhashya' towers supreme; of his expository works, *'Viveka Choodmani'* is prime and of all his works of bhakti, the *Soundaryalahari* tops the list.

Sundaree, the beautiful, is Her name. *Tripura sundari* or *Maha Tripura Sundari* both derived from the root name, *Sundari*, is the Goddess propitiated by the great mantra called *'Shri Vidya'*. Of the many names of *Ambaal*, such as *Parvati, Durga, Kali, Bala, Bhuvaneshvari*, etc., it is the *Sundari* name that goes with *'Raja Rajesvari'*, the Queen name of all the scriptures that talk of and dwell on the Mother Goddess. Sage Ramakrishna has said – I have seen many forms of Gods and Goddesses; but I have never seen one more charming than *'Tripura sundari'*! The word *'Soundaryam'* pertains to Sundari and means 'The Beauty'.

But the beauty of it all is, that the name *'Tripura sundari'* or any of the other (synonymous) names of the same form, namely, *'Lalita'*, *'Raja Rajeshvari'*, *'Kamakshi'* or *'Kaameshvari'* do not occur anywhere in the text, including its title! Even the other descriptive names of the Goddess like *'Hima Giri Suta'* (daughter of Himalaya mountain), or simply, *Giri Sutaa, Shivaa, Bhavanee, Uma, Satee, Parvatee, Chandee* – occur only at one or two places. General attributed names, like '*Jananee*', '*Mataa*', '*Ambaa*', '*Devee*' meaning either 'mother' or 'goddess', – which commonly go with all feminine deities – occur at a few more places, but even they are few.

While he begins with '*Shivaḥ Shaktya*', the most potent name of *Ambaal*, namely '*Shakti*', gets mentioned. 'Shakti' means 'power'. It is the absolute *brahmam*'s power or energy that ambaal personifies. So, this name tells everything about the Goddess. And it comes in the very beginning, but never after.

In sloka no.32, the word 'shakti' appears but there it is a code word for a syllable in *Ambaal's* mantra.

Finally, one more point regarding occurrence of names. The role of a woman has three stages – as daughter, as wife, as mother. The last two roles certainly do get mentioned very often in stotras pertaining to a feminine deity. But the Soundaryalahari uses the daughter reference such as '*Himagiri Sute*', '*Tuhina Giri Kanye*', more often. And again, when the first part of 41 slokas ends, he ends by referring to '*Janaka Jananee*', the mother father role of both *Ishvara* and *Ishvaree* of the whole universe.

Of the 100 sloka s of *Soundaryalahari*, each of them is known to have the curative power against many a disease and mis fortune. While composing the 'Narayaneeyam', Narayana Bhattadri had a humanly incurable disease of the stomach. As he composed his songs, he was sitting in the outer periphery of the sanctum sanctorum, directly leaning to the side and looking in to the Idol of 'Chinna Krishna'. Krishna was giving his approval of each song by nodding his head. At the end of his 'magnum opus' Narayana Bhattadri had no stomach pain and he was fully cured of whatever was the disease. So, chanting of Narayaneeyam, like *Soundaryalahari*, is also used as a curative.

Thus, speaks *Paramācāryā* – Let us bow his lotus feet.

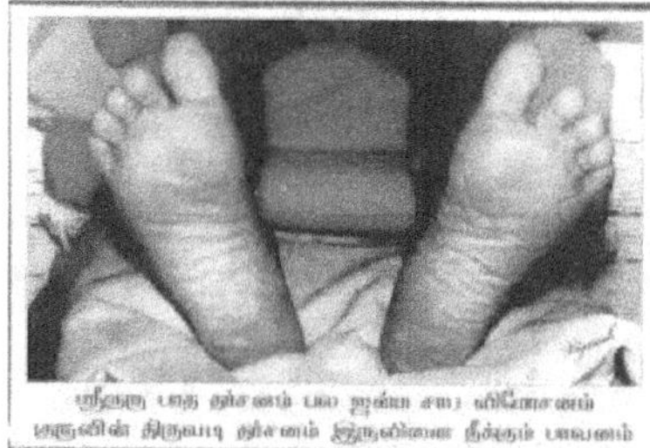

Soundaryalahari – 100 Mantras

The 100 shlokas – verses – *mantras* – are individually discussed in this chapter. The meaning in simple language and wherever possible comparison to other texts like *Lalita Sahasranamam* and all are also provided. The chakras/ *Yantra*s pertaining to each verse alongwith the purpose, result, *Japa* count, number of days the *Japam* to be performed are all also mentioned. The root letters/ *beejaakshara* s inside the *chakras* are mentioned in Tamil. But while performing puja/ *japam* there are to be written in Samskrutam only. These are to be got initiated from an appropriate Guru before starting chanting of *Japams*.

भूमौस्खलित पादानां भूमिरेवा वलम्बनम् ।
त्वयी जाता ऽपराधानां त्वमेव शरणं शिवे ॥

Bhūmauskhalita Pādānām Bhūmirēvā Valambanam I
Tvayī Jātā (A)Parādhānām Tvamēva Śaraṇam Śivē II

The ground itself is the support for the feet that have slipped from the ground. In the same way you alone are the refuge of the offenses born of you, O Shiva!

1. शिव: शक्त्या युक्तो यदि भवति शक्त: प्रभवितुं
   न चेदेवं देवो न खलु कुशल: स्पन्दितुमपि ।
   अतस्त्वाम् आराध्यां हरि हर विरिञ्चादि भिरपि
   प्रणन्तुं स्तोतुं वा कथमकृत पुण्य: प्रभवति ॥

Śivaḥ Śaktyā Yuktō Yadi Bhavati Śaktaḥ Prabhavitum
Na Chēdēvam Dēvō Na Khalu Kuśalaḥ Spanditumapi I
Atastvām Ārādhyām Hari Hara Viriñcādi Bhirapi
Praṇantum Stōtum Vā Kathamakruta Puṇyaḥ Prabhavati II

Lord Shiva, becomes able to do creation and other tasks in this universe, only when is along with *Shakti*. Without her, he cannot move even an inch. In that case how can, one who does not do good deeds, or one who does not sing your praise, become eligible to worship you Oh, Mother! You are worshipped by the trinity Gods.

In *Lalita Sahasranama* 54th name – *Svādheenavallabhā* – One who has a loving and amenable consort. *Shiva's* *shakti* (energy) is *Devee*. Energy is a characteristic feature, which cannot exist on its own, but always exists with matter. Thus, it means that *Shakti* lives with *Shiva* and is obedient to **Her**. But in fact, *Shiva* is controlled by *Shakti* and always seeks **Her** help in all his actions. Although **She** is independent and not under the control of *Parameeśwarā*, **she** is his beloved. *Swādheena* – independent; *Vallabhā* – beloved.

Again, in *Lalita Sahasranama* 410th name – *Shivaparā* – One who is above Lord *Shiva*. Since *Shiva* is owner of *Śreedevee*, **she** is considered above him. **She** has only *Shiva* above **Her**. **She** guides *Shiva* to **Her** devotees.

Again, in *Lalita Sahasranama* 543rd name – *Puṇyalabhyā* – One who can be attained only through virtues/ righteousness. *Puṇya*, good actions performed in previous births – only through this **Her** blessings can be attained.

Again, in *Lalita Sahasranama* 572nd name – *Parāshaktiḥ* – One who is the Supreme energy/ power. Among the elementary substances in the body, skin, blood, flesh, fat and bone were derived from energy (*Shakti*). Marrow, semen, breath and vitality (soul) derived from *Shiva*. The tenth one is called *Parāshakti*.

Parāshakti can also be interpreted as very great energy. (*Parā* – *Utkrushṭa* – very great). The very principle of *Sāktās* is that just by unison with *Shakti*, *Shiva* attains enormous greatness.

Sri Devee Bhāgavatam says, "Only those ever righteous ascetics, who are devoted to wisdom, see; but the men of desire see not the holy and beneficent *Devee*" –

Pashyanti Puṇya Punjā Ye Ye Vedāntas Tapasvinaḥ I
Rāgiṇo Naiva Pashyanti Deveem Bhagavateem Shivām II

Shruti also (*Svetāswara Upanishat* IV 8) says, His supreme *Shakti* is known in different form; *Parāsya Shaktir Vivdhaiva Shrooyate*.

She is also in the *Shakti* form of the *mantra* called *Para*.

Yadi Vā Paścimam Jaṇma Yadi Vā Śaṅkaraḥ Svayam I
Tēṇaiva Labhyatē Vidyā Śrīmatpañcadaśākṣarī II

This is an evidence from *shastras*. Therefore, it is very necessary for those who have attained a very rare human birth to worship *Jagatjanani Parashakti*.

Verse #	1
Yantra with *Beeja* Letters	ॐ श्रीं
Name of the *Yantra*	Sarva Siddhi *Yantra*
Yantra Metal	Gold – *Japam* should be facing East
Japa count #	1,000
# of Days	12
Daily offering	Pure rice
Result	Clearing of obstructions Success in all activities

*****

2. तनीयांसुं पांसुं तव चरण पङ्केरुह भवं
   विरिञ्चिः सञ्चिन्वन् विरचयति लोकान विकलम् ।
   वहत्येनं शौरिः कथमपि सहस्रेण शिरसां
   हरः सङ्क्षुद् यैनं भजति भसितोद्धूलन विधिम् ॥

Tanīyāṃsuṃ Pāṃsuṃ Tava Charaṇa Paṅkēruha Bhavaṃ
Viriñchiḥ Sañchinvan Virachayati Lōkāna Vikalam I
Vahatyēnaṃ Śauriḥ Kathamapi Sahasrēṇa Śirasāṃ
Haraḥ Saṅksud Yainaṃ Bhajati Bhasitōddhūḻana Vidhim II

The grandeur of the dust in the feet of *Śreedevee* has been specially mentioned in the 2nd and 3rd verses of *Soundaryalaharee*.

Lord Brahma, the creator of yore, selects a dust from your lotus feet and creates all the 14 worlds. Lord *Vishnu* in the form of great *Ādisesha* with his thousand heads, somehow carries the dust of your feet, with great effort. Similarly, Lord Rudra, who destroys all the universes during the deluge, claims that the dust of your feet is good and uses it as the holy ash.

In *Lalita Sahasranama* 289th name – *Shruti Seemanta Sindoori Kruta Pādābjadhoolikā* – One who has the dust of **Her** lotus feet forming the vermilion mark on the parting of the hair on the head of the *Vedas*, personified as ladies.

This is a great metaphor. The Deva ladies in the form of *Vedas*, bow to the feet of *Śreedevee*. Thus, the dust in the feet of *Śreedevee* sticks to the head of the ladies (*Vedas*). *Śreedevee*'s feet are decorated with red cotton paste (*mehandi* or henna) and hence the dust is also red in colour. This red colour sticks to the parting of the hair and the meeting point of the forehead and the parting of the hair becomes red. It is a must for the auspicious ladies to wear *Kumkum* at the forehead (start of the parting of the hair). That is the reason they are called *Seemanthinee*. The word *Shruti* (*Vedas*) is also of feminine gender. Hence this metaphor is very apt.

Upanishats are treated as the head of *Vedas*. These are *Gnana Kānda*, which teaches the *Brahmam*. This name relates to *Gnana Kānda*. Hence to indicate the *Brahmam*, *Upanishats* are considered. Even the *Upanishats* are unable to explain the real *Brahmam*, by direct assertions or by complete definition. It is described as this is not, this is not, etc. Hence the word dust is used. The dust in the lotus feet of *Śreedevee* means that the *Vedas* are unable to explain the real form of Devee by direct assertions, by complete definition, describe **Her** by the method of negation, like one ashamed and afraid, standing afar, describing inadequately, that (description also) creates no clear idea as to "this or that". By the word dust, it is described here as the iota of knowledge about *Brahmam*, one can get by adoring *Śreedevee*.

How do we get that ambulatory foot dust when *Śreedevee* is invisible? There is a simple way. According to the scriptures "Striyassamastāḥ Thava Devi Bhedāḥ", on a full moon day, a *Suvasini* (*Sumangali* lady) can be worshiped treating her as *Sri Devi* and her foot dust can be used as Ambal's foot dust. It can be stored safely in a box and worshiped.

Verse #	2
Yantra with *Beeja* Letters	ह्रीं
Yantra Metal	Gold – *Japam* should be facing North
Japa count #	1,000
# of Days	55
Daily offering	Milk Payasam
Result	Attracting the entire world

*****

3. अविद्याना मन्त स्तिमिर मिहिर द्वीपनगरी
जडानां चैतन्य स्तबक मकरन्द श्रुतिझरी ।
दरिद्राणां चिन्तामणि गुणनिका जन्मजलधौ
निमग्नानां दंष्ट्रा मुररिपु वराहस्य भवति ॥

Avidyānā Manta Stimira Mihira Dvīpanagarī
Jaḍānāṃ Chaitanya Stabaka Makaranda Śrutijharī I
Daridrāṇāṃ Chintāmaṇi Guṇanikā Janmajaladhau
Nimagnānāṃ Daṃṣṭrā Muraripu Varāhasya Bhavati II

The dust under your feet, Oh! Goddess great, is like the city of the rising Sun, that removes all darkness. Unfortunately, in the mind of the poor ignorant ones, it is like the honey that flows, from the flower bunch of vital action, to the slow witted one, is like the heap of wish giving gems, to the poorest of men, and is like the teeth of Lord Vishnu in the form of Varāha, who brought to surface, the mother earth, to those drowned in this sea of birth.

In *Lalita Sahasranama* 919th name – *Chaitanya Kusuma Priyā* – One who loves the flower of consciousness (*chaitanya*). The *chaitanya* Itself Is mentioned as a flower here. If it is offered to *Sree Devee*, **she** bestows great results. Consciousness (*chaitanya*) is an intuition. It spreads and comes out through the intellect and mind. When it comes out, through control of senses, it has to be converted into good feelings and offered to *Sree Devee*. The learned people say that there are eight such flowers in *Chaitanya*. They are – non violence, control of senses, compassion, knowledge, penance, truth and meditation. The *chaitanya* containing these eight flowers if very much liked by *Sree Devee*.

171st name in *Sri Lalita Trishati* too – *Hārdasantamasābahā* – Sri Adi Shankara explains   If you want to get rid of illusion, Sri Devi's foot dusts are the only way out. Therefore, devotees who desire Moksha should worship the dusts of feet of *Sri Devi*.

Verse #	3
Yantra with *Beeja* Letters	 श्री
Yantra Metal	Gold – *Japam* should be facing North East

Japa count #	2,000
# of Days	45
Daily offering	Black Gram Vadai
Result	Obtaining all the Vidyas.

*****

4. त्वदन्यः पाणिभ्यामभयवरदो दैवतगणः
त्वमेका नैवासि प्रकटित वराभीत्यभिनया ।
भयात् त्रातुं दातुं फलमपि च वांछासमधिकं
शरण्ये लोकानां तव हि चरणावेव निपुणौ ॥

Tvadanyaḥ Pāṇibhyāmabhayavaradō Daivataganaḥ
Tvamēkā Naivāsi Prakaṭita Varābhītyabhinayā ।
Bhayāt Trātuṃ Dātuṃ Phalamapi Cha Vāñchāsamadhikaṃ
Śaraṇyē Lōkānāṃ Tava Hi Charaṇāvēva Nipuṇau ॥

Śree Ādi Śaṅkara says in his commentary says – without even the emblem of boons in hands, *Śreedevee* provides the boons more than expected to the devotees.

Oh, **she** who is refuge to all this world, all gods except you mother, give refuge and grants wishes, only by their hand. But only you mother never show the world in detail, the boons and refuge that you can give, for even your holy feet will suffice, to remove fear for ever and grant boons much more than asked.

In *Lalita Sahasranama* 331st Name – **Varadā** – One who bestows boons. **She** grants boons to *Brahma, Vishnu* and other devotees. Śree Bhāskararāyar explains what is told by *Nārada* in *Matsya* and *Padma Puranas* –*Śreedevee*'s uplifted hand ever confers boons. **She** will give boons to all *devas, daityas* and ascetics. In reality, the expression means simply to fulfill the desire of the *Devas*; not having the emblem of granthing boons.

Again, in *Lalita Sahasranama* 372nd Name – **Bhakta Mānasahamsikā** – One who is in the form of a swan in the lake like minds of the devotees. The creator, Brahma created a lake, by his mind. It is in the top of mount *Kailash*. Its water is so pure. The swans, which always like purity, live there in an infinite number. It has been described that wherever they travel, during rainy season return to this lake. It has been said in this name as – imaging the pure minds of the devotees to this lake (since it was created by mind, it is called *Mānasa Sarovar* (*Manas* – mind, *Sarovar* – lake) and *Śreedevee* compared to the swans living there.

She is invisible for others, that is, those other than devotees, mount, *ka* is suffixed and mentioned as *Hamsika.*

Again, in *Lalita Sahasranama* 567th Name **– Bhaktanidhiḥ –** One who is a treasure for devotees. **She** offers whatever is asked for by the devotees.

Again, in *Lalita Sahasranama* 795th Name **– Kāmadhuk –** One who fulfills all the desires. **She** fulfills all the desires of **Her** devotees. Fulfilling all the desires is the nature of the celestial cow *Kamdhenu*. **She** is in that form. *Devee Upanishat* also preys; *Sā No Mandreshamoorjam Duhānā Dhenur Vāgasmānupasushtotatitu.*

It can also be meant that **She** is in the form of five *Kāmdughāmbā Devee*s used in *Pancha Panchikā Pooja.*

Again, in *Lalita Sahasranama* 989th Name – **Vānchitārthapradāyinee** – One who bestows what was sought for by the devotees, in plenty. The devotees need not ask for, just thinking is enough. **She** bestows those things. This is clear from the usage of the word *Vānchita.*

Unlike other gods, *Śree Devee* does not have *varada* (bestowing boons) *mudra*. No need for it. According to the Veda sentence – *Mātru Devo Bhava* – *Sri Devi* is an important Goddess. Other Gods(desses) cannot come even near her.

Verse #	4
Yantra with *Beeja* Letters	
Yantra Metal	Gold – *Japam* should be facing East
Japa count #	3,000
# of Days	36
Daily offering	Lemon Rice
Result	To get rid of all types of fears and diseases.

*****

5. हरिस्त्वामाराध्य प्रणत जन सौभाग्य जननीं

पुरा नारी भूत्वा पुररिपुमपि क्षोभ मनयत् ।

स्मरोऽपि त्वां नत्वा रतिनयन लेह्येन वपुषा

मुनीनामप्यन्तः प्रभवति हि मोहाय महताम् ॥

Haristvāmāradhya Praṇata Jana Saubhāgya Jananīṃ
Purā Nārī Bhūtvā Puraripumapi Kṣōbha Manayat I
Smarō'pi Tvāṃ Natvā Ratinayana Lēhyēna Vapuṣā
Munīnāmapyantaḥ Prabhavati Hi Mōhāya Mahatām II

This verse describes the glory of worshipping *Sri Devi*. *Śree Ādi Śaṅkara*, has mentioned that only by the blessings of *Śreedevee*, *Viṣhṇu* took the incarnation as *Mohinee*, to distribute the nectar.

You who grant all the good things, to those who bow at your feet, was worshipped by the Lord Vishnu, who took the pretty lovable feminine form, and could move the mind of he who burnt the cities, and make him fall in love with him. And the God of love, Cupid, took the form which is like nectar, drunk by the eyes of Rathi his wife, after venerating you, was able to create passion, even in the mind of the great sages.

In *Lalita Sahasranama* 298th Name – **Nārāyaṇee** – One who is called as *Nārāyaṇee*. The word *Nara* indicates *Brahmam*. The water is called *nāram*, because it emanated from *Nara* (*Brahmam*). Since *Viṣhṇu* has water as abode (*ayana*), he is named *Nārāyaṇa*. *Nārāyaṇee* is related to him, i.e., his sister. It can also be taken as the word *Nārāyaṇā* indicates *Shiva*. In that case *Nārāyaṇee* is *Shiva*'s consort.

There is no difference between *Nārāyaṇa* and *Śreedevee*. In the form *Arddhānaree*, *Śreedevee* is left half. In the form of *Śaṅkara Nārāyaṇa*, *Nārāyaṇā* is the left half. Hence, they both are one and the same. *Naran* means the soul. The last abode of the souls is *Ayana*. Hence *Nārāyaṇa* also indicates *Shiva*. **She** is the consort of *Shiva*.

Again, in *Lalita Sahasranama* 375th Name – **Kāmapoojitā** – One who was adored by Cupid. *Taitireeya Āraṇyaka* says;
Putro Nirrutyā Vaideha Achetā Yashcha Chetanaḥ Sa Tam Maṇimavindat I

The learned has interpreted this statement as – Cupid, son of *Mahālakshmee*, is without a body, but has attained great knowledge (*Maṇiyai, Panchadasee Vidyā*, etc.). Cupid is one among the 12 great worshippers of *Śreedevee*.

Cupid is also called as *Kāman*. *Kāman* worshipped *Śreedevee* in *Kāncheepuram*. Hence, we see the names *Kāmakottam, Kāmakoṭi* and *Kāmapeeṭam*. These names and the name of *Śreedevee* as *Kamakshi* – having blessed sight on *Kāman*, indicate the greatness of the worship of *Kāman* on *Śreedevee*.

Among the *Peeṭa*s of *Śreedevee* the four important ones are *Kāmagiri Peeṭam*, *Poorṇagiri Peeṭam, Jālandhara Peeṭam* and *Oḍyāna Peeṭam*. *Kāmagiri Peeṭam* is talked about in this name and the remaining discussed in the later names. Considering our body as a *kshetra*, it has to be construed that all the four *peeṭam*s are within the body;

Kāma Peeṭam	– *Moolādhāram*	– the place of *Parā* speech.
Poorṇagiri Peeṭam	– *Maṇipoorakam*	– the place of *Pashyanti* speech.
Jālandhara Peeṭam	– *Anāhatam*	– the place of *Madyamā* speech.
Oḍyāna Peeṭam	– *Vishuddhi*	– the place of *Vaikharee* speech.

Again, in *Lalita Sahasranama* 562nd Name – *Mohinee* – One who is bewitching/ enchanting. *Laghu Nāradeeya Purāṇa* says, **she** makes the entire universe to libidinous with **Her** charming beauty and hence **She** is called as *Mohinee*;

Yasmādidam Jagat Sarvam Tvayā Sundaree Mohitam |
Mohineetyeva Te Nāma Svaguṇottham Bhavishyati ||

It can also be considered as – while churning the milky ocean, *Mahāvishṇu* took the incarnation as *Mohinee* by meditating upon *Śreedevee*. Again, *Śreedevee* took this form. The first one was the form of nature on account of meditating power of *Brahma*. This has been described in *Brahmānḍa Purāṇa*. It has also been mentioned there that *Vishnu* took the *Mohinee* form by meditating upon *Śreedevee*.

The name of the presiding deity in the temple of *Nivāsapura* at the banks of river *Pravarā*, is *Mohinee*.

Again, in *Lalita Sahasranama* 586th Name – *Kāmasevitā* – One who was adored by *Kāma* (cupid). *Kāmā* is *Mahākāmeshvar*. **She** was worshipped by him.

It has been mentioned in *mantra shāstras* that *Mahākāmeshwar* and *Kāmeshwaree* had both mutually taken the role of teacher and student at different times and have given advises mutually. It is very clear from the *Poorva* part that they both have said the *Trishateemantra*.

Kāma indicates the bodiless god of love. *Kādi Vidyā* is one other form of *Panchadasee Vidyā*. *Kāma* is the presiding sage of this *Vidya*. *Sevitā* means a garland of precious gems. This is very clear from the verse starting with;

Manush Chandraḥ Kuberashca Lopāmudrā Ca Manmataḥ ||

As mentioned in the verse – *Haristvām Ārādya* – Let us all realise the real truth, worship Sri Devi and get her complete compassion and be blessed all types of wealth.

Verse #	5
Yantra with *Beeja* Letters	
Yantra Metal	Gold – *Japam* should be facing East
Japa count #	2,000 – keeping the *yantra* on the head
# of Days	8
Daily offering	Dhal Pongal
Result	Attracting others especially ladies

*****

6. धनुः पौष्पं मौर्वी मधुकरमयी पञ्च विशिखाः
वसन्तः सामन्तो मलयमरुदायोधन रथः ।
तथाप्येकः सर्वं हिमगिरिसुते कामपि कृपां
अपाङ्गात्ते लब्ध्वा जगदिद मनङ्गो विजयते ॥

Dhanuḥ Pauṣpaṃ Maurvī Madhukaramayī Pañcha Viśikhāḥ
Vasantaḥ Sāmantō Malayamaru Dāyōdhana Rathaḥ |
Tathāpyēkaḥ Sarvaṃ Himagirisutē Kāmapi Kṛpāṃ
Apāṅgāttē Labdhvā Jagadida Manaṅgō Vijayatē ||

This verse explains the reason for the success of Cupid is the benign look and the blessings of *Śreedevee* only.

You who grant all the good things, to those who bow at your feet, was worshipped by the Lord Vishnu, who took the pretty lovable feminine form, and could move the mind of he who burnt the cities, and make him fall in love with him. And the God of love, Cupid, took the form which is like nectar, drunk by the eyes of Rathi his wife, after venerating you, was able to create passion, even in the mind of Sages the great.

Oh, daughter of the mountain of ice, with a bow made of flowers, bow string made of honey bees, five arrows made of only tender flowers, with spring as his minister, and riding on the chariot of breeze from Malaya mountains the god of love who does not have a body, gets the sideways glance of your holy eyes, and is able to win all the world alone.

Similar to Cupid, every worshipper of Sri Devi will get her compassion through the benign look of her and get all the comforts of the life. There is not even an iota of doubt in this regard.

Verse #	6
Yantra with *Beeja* Letters	क्लीं क्लीं क्लीं साध्यम् क्लीं क्लीं क्लीं
Yantra Metal	Gold – facing East
Japa count #	500
# of Days	21
Daily offering	Sugarcane
Result	Even for a eunuch will get a child

*****

7. क्वणत्काञ्ची दामा करि कलभ कुम्भ स्तननता

परिक्षीणा मध्ये परिणत शरच्चन्द्र वदना ।

धनुर्बाणान् पाशं सृणिमपि दधाना करतलैः

पुरस्ता दास्तां नः पुरमथितु राहो पुरुषिका ॥

Kvaṇatkāñchī Dāmā Kari Kalabha Kumbha Stananatā
Parikṣīṇā Madhyē Pariṇata Śarachchandra Vadanā I

Dhanurbāṇān Pāśaṃ Sṛṇimapi Dadhānā Karatalaiḥ
Purastā Dāstāṃ Naḥ Puramathitu Rāhō Puruṣikā ‖

In this verse, it has been mentioned that She is in the ego form of *Paramashiva*.

With a golden belt, adorned by tiny tingling bells, slightly bent by breasts like the two frontal globes of an elephant fine with a thin pretty form and with a face like the autumn Moon, holding in **her** hands, a bow of sugar cane, arrows made of flowers, and the noose and goad, **she** who has the wonderful form, of the ego of the God who burnt the three cities, should please come and appear before us.

In *Lalita Sahasranama* 312th Name – **Raṇatkinkiṇimekhalā** – One who wears a girdle with tinkling bells.

Again, in *Lalita Sahasranama* 576th Name – **Mattā** – One who is unconscious. She is unconscious due to alcohol in the state of languid/ lethargic. *Mat* indicates self. The thought of self indicates ego.

Verse #	7
Yantra with Beeja Letters	क्रीं
Yantra Metal	Gold or Vibhooti – facing East
Japa count #	1,000
# of Days	12
Daily offering	Rice, Payasam
Result	Attracting kings and enemies

*****

8. सुधासिन्धोर्मध्ये सुरविट पिवाटी परिवृते
मणिद्वीपे नीपो पवनवति चिन्तामणि गृहे ।
शिवाकारे मञ्चे परमशिव पर्यङ्क निलयाम्
भजन्ति त्वां धन्याः कतिचन चिदानन्द लहरीम् ॥

Sudhāsindhōrmadhyē Suravita Pivāṭī Parivṛtē
Maṇidvīpē Nīpō Pavanavati Chintāmaṇi Gṛhē ।
Śivākārē Mañchē Paramaśiva Paryaṅka Nilayām
Bhajanti Tvāṃ Dhanyāḥ Katichana Chidānanda Laharīm ॥

In the middle of the sea of nectar, in the isle of precious gems, which is surrounded by wish giving *Kalpaka* trees, in the garden of *Kadamba* trees, in the house of the gem of thought, on the all holy seat of the lap of the great God Shiva, sits **she** who is like a tide in the sea of happiness of ultimate truth, and is worshipped by only by few select holy men.

In *Lalita Sahasranama* 61st Name – **Sudhāsāgaramadhyasthā** – One who lives in the center of the ocean of nectar. The location of this ocean of nectar is given differently in various sources. According to *Rudryāmalā*, the *Chintāmaṇigraha* is located in this ocean. The *Vedas* say *Yoovaithām Brahmaṇoovedam Amrithenāvratam Purim* (City surrounded by nectar) – *Aruṇa Praśnā* – 27.116. The *Bindusthānā* in the *Chandramaṇḍala*, in the Lotus with thousand petals, below our skull is referred to as *Sudhāsindhu* (Ocean of nectar). According to *Chāndogya Upanishat*, this ocean is located in the city of *Aparājitā*, which can be reached by worshipping a god with attributes (*Saguṇopāsanā*). *Aparājitā* for *Śreedevee* worshippers is like *Kailash* for *Shiva* worshippers and *Śree Vaikuṇṭam* for *Vishnu*'s worshippers. There are two tanks in this city called *Āram* and *Nyam*, which are referred to as *Sudhā Sāgara*.

Hence those who want to lead a healthy long life can worship Sri Devi through this verse.

Verse #	8
Yantra with *Beeja* Letters	
Yantra Metal	Sandal Archana with flowers
Japa count #	1,000
# of Days	12
Daily offering	Pepper Rice, Payasam
Result	Prison related issues, removing the bondage

*****

9. महीं मूलाधारे कमपि मणिपूरे हुतवहं
स्थितं स्वधिष्ठाने हृदि मरुत माकाश मुपरि ।
मनोऽपि भ्रूमध्ये सकलमपि भित्वा कुलपथं
सहस्रारे पद्मे स हरहसि पत्या विहरसे ॥

Mahīm Mūlādhārē Kamapi Maṇipūrē Hutavahaṃ
Sthitaṃ Svadhiṣṭānē Hṛdi Maruta Mākāśa Mupari I
Manō'pi Bhrūmadhyē Sakalamapi Bhitvā Kulapathaṃ
Sahasrārē Padmē Sa Harahasi Patyā Viharasē II

Oh! Goddess, you live in seclusion with your consort, In the lotus with thousand petals, reached after breaking through the micro ways, of the power of earth in *Moolādhāra*, of the power of water of *Maṇipooraka*, of the power of fire of *Swādhishṭāna*, of the fire of air in the heart, and of the power of ether in between the eyelids.

In *Lalita Sahasranama* 90th Name – **Kulāmrutaikarasikā** – One who revels only in *kulāmrutham* – the nectar flowing from the *Sahasrāra*. The subtle form of energy called *Kuṇḍalinee* in every human being is being discussed in this name. The *sushumnā nāḍi* runs from the bottom of the butt, till inner part of the skull through the center of the body along the back bone. In this, the *Kuṇḍalinee* energy sleeps at the bottom tip, in the form of a snake woven itself in three and half rounds, keeping its head in the center downwards. If this *Kuṇḍalinee* energy can be awakened by practicing *Yoga*, it passes through *sushumnā nāḍi* and reaches the inner part of the skull. When this energy bangs with the *Akula Chakra* called *Sahasrārapadmam*, the energy deposited there, melts like butter, seeps, slips down and flows throughout the body as nectar. The nectar thus flows, is called *kulāmrutha*. *Śreedevee* whoops it up in this juice. The common man is able to get only a drop of this *kulāmrutham*. On the other hand, a *yogi* enjoys drenching in the rain of this nectar.

Again, in *Lalita Sahasranama* 106th Name – *Sudhāsārābhivarshiṇee* – *Śreedevee*, seated in the center of *Sahasrāra* Lotus, pelts the nectar to all the *nāḍis* as rainfall from *Chandramaṇḍal*. Reaching this nectar flow and enjoying the indescribable bliss is the sole purpose of this *Upasana*.

Again, in *Lalita Sahasranama* 109th Name – *Mahāsaktiḥ* – The word *Mahā* has two meaning – festival or splendour. *Āsakti* means immense joy. One who is fond of festival (the union of *Shiva* and *Shakti*). One who is very much interested in celebrating offering of prayers as a festival. The word *Mahat* means – so huge expanding to all the directions. **Her** greatness is spread in all directions. **Her** unison is spread in all the places and is visible even in an atom.

Again, in *Lalita Sahasranama* 316th Name – *Ratipriyā* – One who is beloved of *Rati*, the wife of Cupid. *Rati* means copulation and erotic art. For instance, in *Rāmāyana*, *Dasaratha*, after fixing up the crowning of *Rāmā* as prince, went to the palace of *Kaikeyee*. This has been mentioned as *ratyārtham* by *Vālmeekee.*

Thus, the worshippers, after comprehending the philosophies and the forms of the chakras in the body, pray to Sri Devi, will get everything and anything in the life.

The *Chakras* in the human body are identified as in the diagram below with various organs. In *Śrī Lalitā Sahasranāma* it has been mentioned that *Sri Devi* lives in all these *chakra* and *granthis* (knots). Corresponding names are also given;

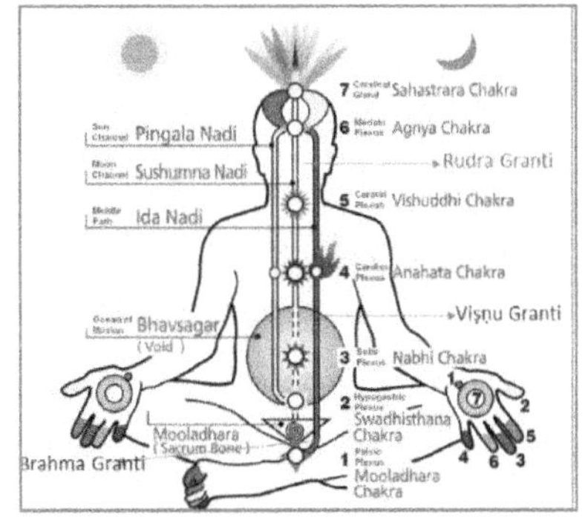

- *Mūlādhāra* – at the base of the back bone at the bottom of the body. 99th name in *Śrī Lalitā Sahasranāma* – *Mūlādhāraikanilayā*.
- *Brahma granthi* in the middle. 100th name in *Śrī Lalitā Sahasranāma* – *Brahma granthivibhedinī*.
- *Svādhiṣṭāna* – at the secret organ. 504th name in *Śrī Lalitā Sahasranāma* – *Svādhishṭānāmbujagatā*.
- *Maṇipūraka* – at the naval. 101st name in *Śrī Lalitā Sahasranāma* – *Maṇipūrāntaruditā*.
- *Viṣṇu granthi* in the middle. 102nd name in *Śrī Lalitā Sahasranāma* – *Viṣṇugranthivibhedinī*.
- *Anāhata* – at the heart. 485th name in *Śrī Lalitā Sahasranāma* – *Anāhatābjanilayā*.
- *Viśuddhi* – at the neck. 475th name in *Śrī Lalitā Sahasranāma* – *ViśuddhiChakra Nilayā*.
- *Rudra granthi* in the middle. 104th name in *Śrī Lalitā Sahasranāma* – *Rudragranthivibhedinī*.

- *Ajnā* – between the eye brows. 103rd name in *Śrī Lalitā Sahasranāma* – *ĀjnāChakrantarālasthā*. In *Śrīmad Bhagavad Gīta* also *Śrī Kriṣṇa* conveys that he resides between the eye brows *'Bruvormadhye'*. This emphasizes the significance of *ĀjnāChakram*.
- *Sahasrāra Chakra* – at the scalp. 105th name in *Śrī Lalitā Sahasranāma* – *Sahasrārāmbujārūḍhā*.

Verse #	9
Yantra with *Beeja* Letters	
Yantra Metal	Gold plate coated with *Kasturi*
Japa count #	1,000
# of Days	45
Daily offering	Milk Payasam
Result	People abroad to return safely. The japam should be facing the direction of the country, which the person has visited

*****

10. सुधाधारासारै श्ररणयुगलान्त विगलितैः
प्रपञ्चं सिन्ज्न्ती पुनरपि रसाम्नाय महसः।
अवाप्य स्वां भूमिं भुजगनिभ मध्युष्ट वलयं
स्वमात्मानं कृत्वा स्वपिषि कुलकुण्डे कुहरिणि ॥

Sudhādhārāsārai Ścharaṇayugalānta Rvigalitaiḥ
Prapañcham Siñcantī Punarapi Rasāmnāya Mahasaḥ ।
Avāpya Svāṃ Bhūmiṃ Bhujaganibha Madhyuṣṭha Valayaṃ
Sva Mātmānaṃ Kṛtvā Svapiṣi Kulakuṇḍē Kuhariṇi ॥

Śree Ādi Śaṇkara, describes, "After reaching your own place, assuming the form of a coiled serpent you sleep in the cavity of the *Kulakuṇḍa*".

Using the nectar that flows in between your feet, to drench all the nerves of the body, and descending from the Moon with nectar like rays, reaching back to your place, and coiling your body in to a ring like serpent. You are sleeping there, which has a small hole, as a wound snake.

In *Lalita Sahasranama* 110th Name – **Kuṇḍalinee** – One who is in the form of *Kuṇḍalinee* energy. **She** is in the form of a serpent coiled in 3.5 rounds. The three rounds respectively represent the letters *A, Uu* and *Ma*. The half round is the half scale. That implies *Kuṇḍalinee* corresponds to *Om* – the *Praṇava mantra*. **She** is breathing like the snake sleeping in *Mooladhāra*. The breath of this *Kuṇḍalinee*, the energy of the soul, is the vital life (*prāṇan*). One can hear the sound of this breath by completely closing the ears. If it is not heard, it is told that death is nearing.

Again, in *Lalita Sahasranama* 440th Name – **Kulakuṇḍālayā** – One who is abiding in the *Kulakuṇḍa*. *Kulakuṇḍa* is the *Bindu*, which is in the center of the pericarp of the *Mooladhāra*. It is like the small cavity in the center of the pericarp of the lotus. **She** has this as **Her** dwelling place. *Kuṇḍalinee* energy always sleeps here by placing its head in the above said cavity, winding three and half times around this *Bindu*.

Ālayam – completely reaching place like *Sushupti*. As mentioned above it is the place for the *kuṇḍalinee* energy and the dwelling place for *Śreedevee*.

Again, in *Lalita Sahasranama* 879th Name – **Sudhāsrutiḥ** – One who is like a stream of nectar. **She** is the ambrosial stream, or flow of bliss, that results from meditation on *Śree Devee* in *sahasrāra*. **She** is the continuous flow of the experience of divine bliss in devoted spiritual practice. The nectar, which is in the Moon of the pericarp of the *Sahasrāra* lotus flower through the *Kuṇḍalini*. The circles of the *Dākini* and other deities are watered by this stream whence the *Kuṇḍalini* becomes the energy of action.

Those who imagine Sri Devi in this form and perform mental worship, she will definitely appear in front of him.

Verse #	10
Yantra with *Beeja* Letters	
Yantra Metal	Gold – *Japam* should be facing East
Japa count #	1,000
# of Days	45

Daily offering	Fruits
Result	Virile development

*****

11. चतुर्भिः श्रीकण्ठैः शिवयुवतिभिः पञ्चभिरपि
प्रभिन्नाभिः शम्भोर्नवभिरपि मूलप्रकृतिभिः ।
चतुश्चत्वारिंशद् वसुदल कलाश्च त्रिवलय
त्रिरेखाभिः सार्धं तव शरणकोणाः परिणताः ॥

Chaturbhiḥ Śrīkaṇṭhaiḥ Śivayuvatibhiḥ Pañchabhirapi
Prabhinnābhiḥ Śambhōrnavabhirapi Mūlaprakṛtibhiḥ I
Chatuśchatvāriṃśad Vasudala Kalāśch Trivalaya
Trirēkhābhiḥ Sārdham Tava Śaraṇakōṇāḥ Pariṇatāḥ II

The geometrical form of Sri Chakra is being explained in this verse.

With four wheels of our Lord Shiva and with five different wheels of you, my mother, which are the real basis of this world, your house of the holy wheel, has four different parts, of eight and sixteen petals, three different circles, and three different lines, making a total of forty four triangles[1].

The angles of Thy abode (the *Śree Chakra*), which is made up of nine *mūlaprakritis* or basic triangles (the nine primary causative forces of the Universe) consisting of the four distinct Shiva triangles (pointing upwards) and five distinct Devee triangles (pointing downwards) kept apart from the former by the Bindu.

Verse #	11
Yantra with *Beeja* Letters	श्रीं
Yantra Metal	Gold plate
Japa count #	1,000

---

[1] There are 4 upward and 5 downward triangles totalling 9. The upward triangles are male/ Shiva triangles and the downward ones are female/ Shakti triangles.

# of Days	8
Daily offering	Jaggery Payasam
Result	To get a child

*****

12. त्वदीयं सौन्दर्यं तुहिनगिरिकन्ये तुलयितुं
कवीन्द्राः कल्पन्ते कथमपि विरिञ्चि प्रभृतयः ।
यदालोकौत्सुक्या दमरललना यान्ति मनसा
तपोभिर्दुष्प्रापामपि गिरिश सायुज्य पदवीम् ॥

Tvadīyaṃ Soundaryaṃ Tuhinagirikanyē Tulayituṃ
Kavīndrāḥ Kalpantē Kathamapi Viriñchi Prabhṛtayaḥ I
Yadālōkautsukyā Damaralalanā Yānti Manasā
Tapōbhirduṣprāpāmapi Giriśa Sāyujya Padavīm II

Oh, Daughter of ice mountain, even the creator who leads, an array of great poets, fail to describe your sublime beauty. The heavenly pretty maidens, with a wish to see your pristine loveliness, try to see you through the eyes of your Lord, the great Shiva, and do penance to him and reach him through their mind.

Oh, daughter of ice mountain, even the creator who leads, an array of great poets, fails to describe your sublime beauty. The heavenly maidens pretty, with a wish to see your pristine loveliness, try to see you through the eyes your Lord, the great *Shiva* and do penance to him and reach him through their mind.

In *Lalita Sahasranama* 48th Name – **Mahālāvaṇyashevadhiḥ** – **She** is a repository or container of all beauty. *Śreedevee*'s divine beauty is unparalleled. **Her** face is described as a container gathering all the beauty.

These nine triangles are called as nine *yonis* and again as nine ores. These nine triangles are comparable with that of six chakras in the human body alongwith three knots. The center *Bindu* is the *Sahasrara* chakra of the body at the top of the head.

Verse #	12	
Yantra with *Beeja* Letters	सौ: सी:	
Yantra Metal	The *chakra* needs to be drawn in water in a cup and at the end can drink the water	
Japa count #	1,000	
# of Days	45	
Daily offering	Honey	
Result	To make the dumb to speak	

*****

13. नरं वर्षीयांसं नयनविरसं नर्मसु जडं
तवापाङ्गालोके पतित मनुधावन्ति शतशः ।
गलद्वेणीबन्धाः कुचकलश विस्त्रिस्त सिचया
हठात् त्रुट्यत्काञ्यो विगलित दुकूला युवतयः ॥

Naraṃ Varṣīyāṃsaṃ Nayanavirasaṃ Narmasu Jaḍaṃ
Tavāpāṅgālōkē Patita Manudhāvanti Śataśaḥ |
Galadvēṇībandhāḥ Kuchakalaśa Vistrista Sichayā
Haṭhāt Truṭyatkāñyō Vigalita Dukūlā Yuvatayaḥ ||

With disheveled hair, with upper cloths slipping from their busts, with the lock of the golden belt getting open due to the haste and with saris slipping away from their shoulders, Hundreds of young lasses, run after the men, who get your sidelong glance, even though they are very old, bad looking and not interested in love sports.

This verse definitively confirms that whoever is blessed to get Sri Devi's benign look, attains the ultimate bliss.

Verse #	13
Yantra with *Beeja* Letters	क्रीं क्रीं क्रीं साध्यम् क्रीं क्रीं क्रीं
Yantra Metal	Lead or Gold plate
Japa count #	1,000
# of Days	45
Daily offering	3 sweet substances, rice
Result	Attracting ladies

*****

14. क्षितौ षट्पञ्चाशद् द्विसमधिक पञ्चाश दुदके
हुताशे द्वाषष्टि श्चतुरधिक पञ्चाश दनिले ।
दिवि द्विः षट् त्रिंशत् मनसि च चतुःषष्टिरिति ये
मयूखा स्तेषा मप्युपरि तव पादाम्बुज युगम् ॥

Kṣitau Ṣaṭpañchāśad Dvisamadhika Pañchāśa Dudakē
Hutāśē Dvāṣaṣṭi Śchaturadhika Pañchāśa Danilē |
Divi Dviḥ Ṣaṭ Trimśat Manasi Cha Chatuḥṣaṣṭiriti Yē
Mayūkhā Stēṣā Mapyupari Tava Pādāmbuja Yugam ||

It has been mentioned that there are 64 *Tantras. Śreedevee* has all these as **Her** form.

Your two holy feet are far above, the fifty six rays of the essence of earth of *Moolādhāra*, the fifty two rays of the essence of water of *Maṇipooraka*, the sixty two rays of the essence of fire of *Swādhishṭāna*, the fifty four rays of the essence of air of *Anāhata*, the seventy two rays of the essence of ether of *Vishuddhi*, and the sixty four rays of the essence of mind of *Agna chakra*.

In *Lalita Sahasranama* 236th Name – **Chatushshashtikalāmayee** – One who embodies the sixty four forms of arts. **She** has all the arts in **Her** form. *Kalā* also means *Tantra*. It has been mentioned that there are sixty four arts. But there are differences in views while listing down the 64 arts. The below list is as given by *Bhāskara Rāya;*

1. The knowledge of the scripts of eighteen languages – Samskrutam, *Prakrut, Udeechi, Mahārashtree, Magatee, Mishramāgatee, Chakāpeeri, Avanti, Drāvedee, Otriyā, Pāchādyā, Prāchyā, Bāhveekā, Rantikā, Dākshinādyā, Paichachee, Āvantee* and *Chourasenee.*
2. Writing these scripts.
3. The power of writing and reading these languages quickly.
4. Drawing
5. Knowledge of different languages
6. Composing verses in them
7. The art of repeating what is heard.
8. Gambling
9. 9 to 12 – Knowledge of the four *Vedas* – *Rig, Yajur, Sāma* and *Atharvana*
13. 13 to 16 – Knowledge of the four auxiliary *Vedas* – *Gāndharvā, Ayur Veda, Danur Veda* and *Artha Shāstra.*
17. 17 to 22 – Knowledge of six *sastras* – *Nyāsa, Vaiseshikā, Sānkhyā, Yoga, Meemamsā* and *Vedanta.*
23. 23 to 28 Knowledge of six *vedāngās* – *Shikshā, Vyākaranā, Chandas, Nruktā, Jyothishā* and *Kalpa.*
29. Knowledge of *Tantras, Puranas* and *Smrutees*
30. Knowledge of poetry, rhetoric and drama
31. 31 to 36 Knowledge of pacifying, controlling, attracting, enmity, ruining by magical practices, and killing
37. 37 to 43 The art of opposing the effects of motion, water, sight, fire, weapons, speech, and semen
44. The art of making scriptures
45. 45 to 48 Art of training elephants, horses, chariots and men
49. The knowledge of divination by bodily marks (*sāmudrikā*)
50. Art of boxing
51. Art of cooking
52. Art of removing venom
53. Art of playing string instruments
54. Art of playing wind instruments like flute
55. Art of playing percussion instruments
56. Art of playing heavy instruments made of bronze.
57. Creating illusion (*Indrajāla*)
58. Art of dancing
59. Art of singing
60. The art of alchemy
61. Knowledge of testing gems
62. Thieving

63.   Knowledge of the pulse
64.   Art of disappearance

Your two holy feet are far above, the fifty six rays of the essence of Earth of *Mooladhara*, the fifty two rays of the essence of water of *Manipooraka*, the sixty two rays of the essence of fire of *Swadhishtana*, the fifty four rays of the essence of air of *Anahata*, the seventy two rays of the essence of Ether of Vishuddhi and the sixty four rays of the essence of mind of Agna chakra.

Verse #	14
Yantra with *Beeja* Letters	
Yantra Metal	Gold plate
Japa count #	1,000
# of Days	45
Daily offering	Milk Payasam
Result	Healthy life without hunger disease

*****

15. शरज्ज्योत्स्ना शुद्धां शशियुत जटाजूट मकुटां
वर त्रास त्राण स्फटिकघटिका पुस्तक कराम् ।
सकृन्न त्वा नत्वा कथमिव सतां सन्निदधते
मधु क्षीर द्राक्षा मधुरिम धुरीणाः फणितयः ॥ 15

Śarajjyōtsnā Śuddhāṃ Śaśiyuta Jaṭājūṭa Makuṭāṃ
Vara Trāsa Trāṇa Sphaṭikaghaṭikā Pustaka Karām ।
Sakṛnna Tvā Natvā Kathamiva Satāṃ Sannidadhatē
Madhu Kṣīra Drākṣā Madhurima Dhurīṇāḥ Phaṇitayaḥ ॥

Sweetest words rivaling the honey, milk and grapes, can only come the thoughts of the devotee, who once meditates on your face, which is like the white autumn Moon, on your head with a crown with the crescent Moon and flowing hair, and hands that shower boons and give protection, which hold the crystal chain of beads and books. This verse is inter related with next two verses.

Verse #	15
Yantra with *Beeja* Letters	
Yantra Metal	Gold plate or write in water and drink it after japam
Japa count #	1,000
# of Days	45
Daily offering	Honey, sugar, fruits
Result	Poetry, Music

*****

16. कवीन्द्राणां चेतः कमलवन बालातप रुचिं
भजन्ते ये सन्तः कतिचिदरुणामेव भवतीम् ।
विरिञ्चि प्रेयस्या स्तरुणतर श्रृङ्गार लहरी
गभीराभि र्वाग्भिः विदधति सतां रञ्जनममी ॥

Kavīndrāṇāṃ Chētaḥ Kamalavana Bālātapa Ruchiṃ
Bhajantē Yē Santaḥ Katichidaruṇāmēva Bhavatīm ।
Viriñchi Prēyasyā Staruṇatara Śṛṅgāra Laharī
Gabhīrābhi Rvāgbhiḥ Rvidadhati Satāṃ Rañjanamamī ॥ 16

She who is the purple luster of the dawn, to the lotus forest like mind, of the kings of poets of the world, and thus called *Aruna* – the purple coloured one, creates happiness in the mind of the holy, tender passionate wave of words, which are royal and youthful.

In *Lalita Sahasranama* 505th Name – **Chaturvaktramanoharā** – One who is fascinating with **Her** four faces. *Svādhishṭāna* is the place of water. Hence starting from ether until water the four primary elements represent the four faces of *Śreedevee*.

Again, in *Lalita Sahasranama* 798th Name – ***Kāvyakalā*** – One who is the poetic art. *Kāvyā*, the work of poets, which is divided into various types, namely poems, drama, etc. They all originate from sounds and words. **She** is in those forms. It can also be said that **She** is in the form creating the above said arts and the corresponding ability.

To write a poem, a creative thought has to originate. By worshipping *Sreedevee* in a particular manner, she blesses with the ability of creating poems.

Those who chant this verse, imagine and mentally worship *Aruna Devi* in the lotus heart, would definitely be blessed by Goddess Saraswathi.

Verse #	16
Yantra with *Beeja* Letters	वं वं वं
Yantra Metal	Gold plate
Japa count #	1,000
# of Days	45
Daily offering	Honey
Result	Knowledge of all the four Vedas

*****

17. सवित्रीभि र्वाचां चशि मणि शिला भङ्ग रुचिभि

वशिन्यद्याभि स्त्वां सह जननि सञ्चिन्तयति यः ।

स कर्ता काव्यानां भवति महतां भङ्गिरुचिभि

र्वचोभि र्वाग्देवी वदन कमलामोद मधुरैः ॥

Savitrībhi Rvāchāṃ Chaśi Maṇi Śilā Bhaṅga Ruchibhi
Rvaśinyadyābhi Stvāṃ Saha Janani Sañchintayati Yaḥ I
Sa Kartā Kāvyānāṃ Bhavati Mahatāṃ Bhaṅgiruchibhi
Rvachōbhi Rvāgdēvī Vadana Kamalāmōda Madhuraiḥ II

Oh, holy mother, he who worships you, along with the goddesses like Vasinee, who are the prime source of words, and you who are having the great luster, got by breaking the Moon stone, becomes the author of great epics, which shine like those written by great ones, and which have the sweet scent of the face of the goddess of knowledge.

In *Lalita Sahasranama* 613th Name – **Kāvyālāpavinodinee** – One who gets delighted with poetical speech, dialogue, description, etc. The books written by poets are called *kāvyās*. Eighteen characteristics have been declared for a *kāvya*. It is told that the story of *Rama* written by sage *Vālmiki* is the oldest *kāvya*. **She** gets very much pleased specially by such *kāvyās*.

The characters of a *kāvyā* have been described as – *Vākyam Rasātmakam Kāvyam* and *Ramaneeyartthapratipādakaḥ Shabdaḥ Kāvyam*. Accordingly, **she** enjoys *kāvyās* and its characters like the flavour of the descriptions, rhetoric speech, figures of speech, etc.

A devotee who worships *Śreedevee* methodically gets the capability of writing *kāvyās*. For instance, *Kālidāsa*, *Mookha* and others.

This verse alongwith the *Srisookta mantra* starting from '*Gandadvārām*' has to be chant and Sri Devi has to be imagined in Sri Chakra and worshipped.

Verse #	17
Yantra with *Beeja* Letters	
Yantra Metal	Gold plate
Japa count #	1,000
# of Days	45
Daily offering	Honey, milk, Sugarcane, Sugar
Result	Knowledge of all the *shastras*

*****

18. तनुच्छायाभिस्ते तरुण तरणि श्रीसरणिभि:
दिवं सर्वां उर्वीं अरुणिम निमग्नां स्मरति य: ।

भवन्त्यस्य त्रस्य द्वनहरिण शालीन नयनाः
सहोर्वश्या वश्याः कति कति न गीर्वाण गणिकाः ॥

Tanuchchāyābhistē Taruṇa Taraṇi Śrīsaraṇibhi
Rdivaṃ Sarvā Murvī Maruṇima Nimagnāṃ Smarati Yaḥ ǀ
Bhavantyasya Trasya Dvanahariṇa Śālīna Nayanāḥ
Sahōrvaśyā Vaśyāḥ Kati Kati Na Gīrvāṇa Gaṇikāḥ ǁ

He who meditates on, the luster of your beautiful body, which is in the colour of the rising sun and which dissolves the sky and the world, in light purple hue, makes celestial damsels like *Urvashi* and others, who have eyes like the wild startled deer, follow like slaves.

Verse #	18
Yantra with *Beeja* Letters	
Yantra Metal	Gold plate – sandal, Kumkum, flowers
Japa count #	1,000
# of Days	45
Daily offering	Payasam, milk, petal leaves
Result	Art of speech, attracting ladies

*****

19. मुखं बिन्दुं कृत्वा कुचयुगमध स्तस्य तदध:
हरार्धं ध्यायेद्य: हरमहिषि ते मन्मथकलाम् ।
स सद्य: सङ्क्षोभं नयति वनिता इत्यतिलघु
त्रिलोकीमप्याशु भ्रमयति रवीन्दु स्तनयुगाम् ॥

Mukhaṃ Binduṃ Kṛtvā Kuchayugamadha Stasya Tadadhō
Harārdhaṃ Dhyāyēdyō Haramahiṣi Tē Manmathakalām ǀ
Sa Sadyaḥ Saṅkṣōbhaṃ Nayati Vanitā Ityatilaghu
Trilōkīmapyāśu Bhramayati Ravīndu Stanayugām ǁ

Hey, Mother who is Goddess of all universe, he who meditates on you, as the crescent of love of our lord great, on the dot of the holy wheel, your two busts just below, and you as the half of Shiva our lord, not only creates waves of emotion in ladies, but charms the world, which has Moon and Sun as busts.

In *Lalita Sahasranama* 322nd Name – **Kāmakalāroopā** – One who is in the form of *Kāmakala*. There are three *bindus* (one above and two in the sides) and the *hārdakalā*, in a triangle form at the bottom. This is described by the letter '*Em*'. It is very clear from *tantra shāstras* that this indicates the union of *Shiva* and *Shakti*. The first *bindu* is called *kāmā* and the *hārdakalā* is called as *kalā*. According to the rule of *Pratyāhāra* of Samskrutam, *Kāmakāla* includes all the four.

The real nature of *Kāmakalā* is set forth in the book called *Kāmakalāvilāsa*. Also, in the *tantra* books like *Sāradā Tilakam*, *Prapanchasāram*, etc.

Again, in *Lalita Sahasranama* 712th Name – **Ee** – One who is in the form of *Ĕ*, the *Kāmakalā* letter. '*Ĕ*' is the 4th of the 16 vowels in Samskrutam. The first letter *A* indicates *Vishnu*. His sister *Śreedevee* is indicated by the 4th letter. The combined form of these two is indicated by *A + Ĕ = AE* can be seen in 715th name. This is based on the grammar rule viz., *Yasyeti Cha*.

According to *Śree Vidyā* practice this letter indicates the *kāmakala*. Its form has been described in *Vāmkesvara Tantra*, *Gnānārnavam*, *Vayu Puranam*, *Kāmakalā Vilāsam*. This is *Śreedevee*'s subtle form.

Again, in *Lalita Sahasranama* 905th Name – **Baindavāsanā** – One who is seated on *Bindu*. The *bindu*, called as *Sarvānandamaya Chakra*, in the center of the triangle in the middle of the *Śree Chakra*. This is called *Baindava* place. **She** resides there. The *Baindava* resembles the round spot above the eye brows. The *Svacchaṇḍa Tantra* says, above the *Hākini* circle there is a disc called *Bindu*; *Hākinee Maṇḍalādoordhvam Bindu Roopam Tu Vartulam*. There, after describing the lotus and *Shiva*, there is the energy *Manonmaṇi*, which is above the *Shanti*, on the left side, etc.";

Vāmabāge Samāseenā shāntryateetā Manonmanee ॥

In addition, *Bindu* indicates the below seats and **She** dwells in all these.

   a.   *Sudhā Sindu*
   b.   The Moon's disc in the *karnikā* of *Sahasrāra Kamala*.

c.   The lap of *Kāmeshwara*.

She has the collection of bindus, as her seat or form. **She** is the support for all those indicate by these words. It can also be considered as the *Kāmakala* form of *Śree Devee*.

Verse #	19
Yantra with *Beeja* Letters	
Yantra Metal	Gold plate – Vibhooti, sandal, Kumkum
Japa count #	1,000
# of Days	25
Daily offering	Milk Payasam, Honey
Result	Attracting Kings, ladies and animals

*****

20. किरन्ती मङ्गेभ्यः किरण निकुरुम्बामृतरसं
हृदि त्वा माधत्ते हिमकरशिला मूर्तिमिव यः ।
स सर्पाणां दर्प शमयति शकुन्ताधिप इव
ज्वरप्लुष्टान् दृष्ट्या सुखयति सुधाधारसिरया ॥

Kirantī Maṅgēbhyaḥ Kiraṇa Nikurumbāmṛtarasaṃ
Hṛdi Tvā Mādhattē Himakaraśilā Mūrtimiva Yaḥ I
Sa Sarpāṇāṃ Darpaṃ Śamayati Śakuntādhipa Iva
Jvarapluṣṭān Dṛṣṭyā Sukhayati Sudhādhārasirayā II

He who meditates in his mind, on you who showers nectar from all your limbs and in the form, which resembles, the statue carved out of moonstone, can with a single stare, put an end to the pride of snakes and with his nectar like vision, cure those afflicted by fever.

Hence, the devotees can chant this verse, at least 100 times a day and worship *Sri Devi*. They will be warded off from all kinds of diseases and lead a healthy long life.

Verse #	20
Yantra with *Beeja* Letters	
Yantra Metal	Gold plate or water
Japa count #	1,000
# of Days	25
Daily offering	Milk Payasam
Result	To keep off evil eyes, poisonous fever

*****

21. तटिल्लेखा तन्वीं तपन शशि वैश्वानर मयीं
निषण्णां षण्णामप्युपरि कमलानां तव कलाम् ।
महापद्माटव्यां मृदित मलमायेन मनसा
महान्तः पश्यन्तो दधति परमाह्लाद लहरीम् ॥

Taṭillēkhā Tanvīṃ Tapana Śaśi Vaiśvānara Mayīṃ
Niṣaṇṇāṃ Ṣaṇṇāmapyupari Kamalānāṃ Tava Kalāṃ I
Mahāpadmāṭavyāṃ Mṛdita Malamāyēna Manasā
Mahāntaḥ Paśyantō Dadhati Paramāhlāda Laharīm II

Those souls great, who have removed all the dirt from the mind and meditate on you within their mind, who is of the form of sun and moon and living in the forest of lotus and also above the six wheels of lotus, enjoy waves after waves, of happiness supreme.

This verse is an apt tool for devotees' life be filled with happiness, devoid of sorrows.

Verse #	21
Yantra with *Beeja* Letters	
Yantra Metal	Gold or silver plate
Japa count #	1,000
# of Days	11
Daily offering	Honey, fruits
Result	To keep off others' anger

*****

22. भवानि त्वं दासे मयि वितर दृष्टिं सकरुणां
इति स्तोतुं वाञ्छन् कथयति भवानि त्वमिति यः ।
तदैव त्वं तस्मै दिशसि निजसायुज्य पदवीं
मुकुन्द ब्रह्मेन्द्र स्फुट मकुट नीराजितपदाम् ॥

Bhavāni Tvaṃ Dāsē Mayi Vitara Dṛṣṭiṃ Sakaruṇāṃ
Iti Stōtuṃ Vāñchan Kathayati Bhavāni Tvamiti Yaḥ ।
Tadaiva Tvaṃ Tasmai Diśasi Nijasāyujya Padavīṃ
Mukunda Brahmēndra Sphuṭa Makuṭa Nīrājitapadām ॥

In this *verse*, assuming two usages for the word *Bhavani* the grace of *Śreedevee* is explained. The word *Bhavani* is used as an exclamation and as a predicate.

A devotee thinks to address *Śreedevee* as *Bhavani*! and ask **Her** – why can't you pass your graceful sight on the slave like me? In this regard the devotee just starts with the two words "*Bhavani* You" – Instantly *Śreedevee* takes the request as "I have to become you". **She** provides the salvation, which is rare even for the *Devas* including *Brahma*.

In *Lalita Sahasranama* 112th Name – **Bhavānee** – The word *Bhava* has three meanings – Lord *Mahadeva*, the human life cycle and Cupid. **She** gives life (*Ānayathee*) to all these three and hence *Bhavānee*. Since Lord *Paramashiva* creates all the living things his name is *Bhava*. His consort is *Bhavānee*. Out of the eight forms of Lord *Paramashiva*, the form of water is called *Bhava*. His consort is *Bhavānee*. One who gives life to the living form of water is *Bhavānee*. (*Tayonmruḍa Jeevase – Śree Rudra* verse can also be reminded). The name of *Śreedevee* in Sthaneshwara Shetra is *Bhavānee*.

The great Veda sentence '*Tatvamasi*' and this verse communicate the same sense.

Verse #	22
Yantra with *Beeja* Letters – (*Sri Chakram*)	
Yantra Metal	Gold – in a temple or banks of a holy river
Japa count #	1,000
# of Days	45
Daily offering	Mixed rice
Result	Getting king's post

*****

23 त्वया हृत्वा वामं वपु रपरितृप्तेन मनसा
शरीरार्धं शम्भो: अपरमपि शङ्के हृतमभूत् ।
यदेतत् त्वद्रूपं सकलमरुणाभं त्रिनयनं
कुचाभ्यामानम्रं कुटिल शशिचूडाल मकुटम् ॥

Tvayā Hṛtvā Vāmaṃ Vapu Raparitṛptēna Manasā
Śarīrārdhaṃ Śambhōḥ Aparamapi Śaṅkē Hṛtamabhūt ।
Yadētat Tvadrūpaṃ Sakalamaruṇābhaṃ Trinayanaṃ
Kuchābhyāmānamram Kuṭila Śaśichūḍāla Makuṭam ॥

This is the message *Paramāchārya* has communicated that in the *Ardhanāreeshvara* form the left half belongs to *Shakti* and the right half belongs to Shiva. Hence the left half is expected to be red in colour and the right half should be white in colour. But the entire body of *Shreedevee* is red in colour. And hence arises a doubt in me, that you were not satisfied, by half the body of *Shambu* that he gave, and occupied all his body –
Shareeram Tvam Shambhoḥ ।

Oh! Goddess supreme, I always see in my mind's eye, that your body with Sun and Moon, as busts is the body of Shiva, and his peerless body with nine surrounding motes, is your body, my goddess. And hence the relation of, "that which has", and "he who has", Becomes the one perfect relation of happiness, and becomes equal in each of you –

Shivayuvathi Bhāvena Bibhrushe |

There is nothing accept you in the world, but to make believe your form as the universe, you take the role of wife of Shiva, and appear before us in the form of ethereal happiness –

Shivam Seve Deveemapi Shivasamāna Vyvasitām |

I bow before the Shiva, who is of the pure crystal form, in thine supremely pure wheel and who creates the principle of ether, and to you my mother, who has same stream of thought as Him. I bow before you both.

In *Lalita Sahasranama* 122nd Name – **Shāmbhavee** – Consort of *Shambu*. Mother of devotees of Lord *Shiva*. *Shāmbhavee Devee* is mentioned in *Śree Vidyāratna Sūtra*s of *Śree Gowḍapādar.* This has been described in detail in the commentary as; Nobleness of mind (*Satva Guṇa* form), white in colour, consort of *Rudra*, creator of *uttarāmnāya mantra*s in the form of *Sāma Veda,* etc.

During festival days like *Navarātri*, during *Navāvarṇa Pooja* and at the end of *Chaṇḍi Homa*, worship is done on *Sumangali* (auspicious ladies with husband), young girls (*kanyā*) and young boys (*brahmacāri*).

Again, in *Lalita Sahasranama* 392nd Name – **Shreekanṭhārdhashareeriṇee** – One who has a body constituting one half of *Shiva*. The word *Shree* has venom as a meaning. Since Lord *Paramashiva* has venom in his neck, he got the name as *Shreekanṭan* (*kanṭam* – neck). **She** has *Paramashiva* as **Her** half body or **She** has in differentiable half body with *Paramashiva*.

Again, in *Lalita Sahasranama* 861st Name – **Kāntārdhavigrahā** – One who has the half body of her consort. *Ardhanāri* form is being considered here. It can be taken in two ways – **She** has taken half body of *Parameshwara* or He has taken half body of **Hers**. Both are correct according to grammar.

The end of letter *ka* is *kha*. *Kha* means heaven. Heaven is also a part of **Her** body. *Chāndogya Upanishat* (III 12 6) describes – all the living beings are one fourth of **Her** only and other three immortal portions are in the heaven –

Pādosya Sarvā Bhootāni Tripadasyāmrutam Diveeti |

In *Lalita Trishatee* also 52nd Name also conveys the same message – **Eeśvarārdhāṅgaśareerā** – One who has *Eeshvar* as half of her body – Who forms the (left) half of the body of Parmeshwar – Whose half body is composed of the body of Eshwar. This name can be been interpreted as –

- **Her** body is in the form of *Ānanda*. The letter '*Ha*' in Samskrutam indicates *Eshvar*. **She** is that half body of *Eeshvar* i.e., **She** is in the form of the letter '*E*' in Samskrutam as *Shakti Beeja*. The letter '*Ha*' can also be written as ':' (*visarga*). In some schools it is mentioned that **She** is half of it (*Anusvāram*).
- *Brahadāraṇya Upanishat* (verses I–3, 1–4) explains the universal absolute (*Parabrahmam*) becoming two as husband and wife – starting from *Ātmaivedamagra Āseet* till *Sa Imamevātmānam Dvetā'bhātayat Tataḥ |*
- It is mentioned in the *Vayu Purana* as; Lord *Paramashiva's* body is white in colour whereas his neck is black (on account venom). Similarly, *Sree Devee's* body is partly in the form of *Gowri*, which is white in colour and partly in the form of *Kālee*, who is black in colour.

Verse #	23
Yantra with *Beeja* Letters	
Yantra Metal	Gold plate
Japa count #	1,000
# of Days	45
Daily offering	Payasam, Black gram Vadai
Result	To get rid of loans, to get wealth

*****

24. जगत्सूते धाता हरिरवति रुद्रः क्षपयते
तिरस्कुर्व न्नेतत् स्वमपि वपु रीश स्तिरयति ।
सदा पूर्वः सर्व तदिद मनुगृह्णाति च शिव
स्तवाज्ञां आलम्ब्य क्षणचलितयो भ्रूलतिकयोः ॥

Jagatsūtē Dhātā Hariravati Rudraḥ Kṣapayatē
Tiraskurva Nnētat Svamapi Vapu Rīśa Stirayati |

Sadā Pūrvaḥ Sarvaṃ Tadida Manugrhṇāti Cha Śiva
Stavājjñām Āalambya Kṣaṇachalitayō Rbhrūlatikayōḥ ॥

She issues those orders just by twinkling her eye brows for a micro second. *Brahma* creates the universe, *Viṣhṇu* protects it and *Rudra* destroys it. *Shiva* annihilates all these three as well as himself and finally, under thy order indicated by the movement of thy creepers like brows, *Sadāshiva* approves the same.

In *Lalita Sahasranama* 274th Name – **Panchakrutyaparāyaṇā** – One who is devoted to the five functions. **She** has much interest and involvement in all the five tasks. It can also be interpreted that all the five functions depend on **Her**. The five functions viz. creation, protection, destruction, annihilation, and causing the appearance of the universe are that of *Brahma, Vishnu, Rudra, Eshwar* and *Paramashiva.* These five are different forms or *Shaktis* of that *Śreedevee* only. The officials of these five functions carry out their tasks with the permission of *Śreedevee* only. It is **Her** order to make them do these functions.

Again, in *Lalita Sahasranama* 995th Name – **Sarvānullanghyashāsana** – One whose commands cannot be disobeyed by anybody. **She** is understood by learned and lay men as well. However, nobody can exploit the nearness and disobey **Her** orders. Even the three Gods *Brahma, Viṣhṇu* and *Rudra* understand the commands of *Śree Devee* just by her blinking of eye brows and execute the same.

Verse #	24
Yantra with *Beeja* Letters	न शि य म: खा य म: खा न शि खा न शि य म: शि य म: खा न म: खा न शि य
Yantra Metal	Gold plate
Japa count #	1,000
# of Days	45
Daily offering	Honey, Black gram Vadai, Sweet till rice
Result	To get rid of all types of voodooism.

*****

25. त्रयाणां देवानां त्रिगुण जनितानां तव शिवे
भवेत् पूजा पूजा तव चरणयो र्या विरचिता ।
तथा हि त्वत्पादोद्वहन मणिपीठस्य निकटे
स्थिता ह्येते शश्वन्मुकुलित करोत्तंस मकुटाः

Trayāṇām Dēvānāṃ Triguṇa Janitānāṃ Tava Śivē
Bhavēt Pūjā Pūjā Tava Charaṇayō Ryā Virachitā ।
Tathā Hi Tvatpādōdvahana Maṇipīṭhasya Nikaṭē
Sthitā Hyētē Śaśvanmukulita Karōttaṃsa Makuṭhāḥ ॥

Oh! consort of Shiva! the worship done at the base of your feet, is the worship done to the holy Trinity, born based on your trine properties. This is so true, Oh mother! because don't the Trinity, always stand with folded hands, kept on their crown near the jeweled plank, which carries thine feet.

The six source *chakras* in the body are the pedestals of Sri Devi. They are divided into pair of *chakras* – Agni, Sun and Moon. Brahma, Vishnu and Rudra reside in the three *granthis* (knots) of the respective pairs. Therefore, the devotee internally worshiping Sri Devi in all the six chakras results in worshipping Brahma, Vishnu and Rudra also.

Verse #	25
Yantra with *Beeja* Letters	सौः
Yantra Metal	Gold plate
Japa count #	1,000
# of Days	45
Daily offering	Honey
Result	To come to power

*****

26. विरिञ्चिः पञ्चत्वं व्रजति हरिराप्नोति विरतिं
विनाशं कीनाशो भजति धनदो याति निधनम् ।

वितन्द्री माहेन्द्री विततिरपि संमीलित दृशा
महासंहारेऽस्मिन् विहरति सति त्वत्पति रसौ ॥

Viriñchiḥ Pañchatvaṃ Vrajati Harirāpnōti Viratiṃ
Vināśaṃ Kīnāśō Bhajati Dhanadō Yāti Nidhanam ।
Vitandrī Māhēndrī Vitatirapi Sammīlita Dṛśā
Mahāsaṃhārē'smin Viharati Sati Tvatpati Rasau ॥

Shiva does not perish just because of the pride of your earrings only, says *Śree Ādi Śaṇkara*. The creator reaches the dissolution, the Vishnu attains death, the god of death even dies, Kubera the lord of wealth expires, the Indras close their eyes one after one, and attain the wakeless sleep, during the final deluge. But you my chaste mother, play with your consort the *Sadāshiva*.

In *Lalita Sahasranama* 571st Name – **Mahāpralayasākshiṇee** – One who is the witness of the great dissolution. As the entire universe perish at the time of the great dissolution. *Brahma* and *Vishnu* also merge with *Śreedevee*. A witness is that person who does not participate in the action, is not affected by the fruit of it, and completes seeing the action. **She** is such a witness to the great dissolution.

The creator reaches the dissolution, the Vishnu attains the end, the god of death even dies, Kubera the lord of wealth expires, the Indras close their eyes one after one and attain the wake less sleep, during the final deluge. But you my chaste Mother, play with your consort the *Sadashiva*.

Verse #	26
Yantra with *Beeja* Letters	
Yantra Metal	Gold or lead plate
Japa count #	1,000
# of Days	11 New Moon days
Daily offering	Sugar Pongal
Result	To get rid of enemies

*****

27. जपो जल्पः शिल्पं सकलमपि मुद्राविरचना
गतिः प्रादक्षिण्य क्रमण मशनाद्याहुति विधिः ।
प्रणामः संवेशः सुखमखिल मात्मार्पण दृशा
सपर्या पर्याय स्तव भवतु यन्मे विलसितम् ॥

Japō Jalpaḥ Śilpaṃ Sakalamapi Mudrāvirachanā
Gatiḥ Prādakṣiṇya Kramaṇa Maśanādyāhuti Vidhiḥ I
Praṇāmaḥ Saṃvēśaḥ Sukhamakhila Mātmārpaṇa Dṛśā
Saparyā Paryāya Stava Bhavatu Yanmē Vilasitam II

Let the mutterings that I do, with the sacrifice in my soul, become chanting of your name. Let all my movements become thine Mudras. Let my travel become perambulations around thee. Let the act of eating and drinking become fire sacrifice to thee. Let my act of sleeping becomes salutations to you. And let all actions of pleasure of mine, become parts of thine worship.

Verse #	27
Yantra with *Beeja* Letters	
Yantra Metal	Gold plate
Japa count #	1,000
# of Days	45
Daily offering	Milk
Result	To get self realisation

*****

28. सुधामप्यास्वाद्य प्रति भय जरामृत्यु हरिणीं
विपद्यन्ते विश्वे विधि शतमखाद्या दिविषदः ।
करालं यत्क्ष्वेलं कबलितवतः कालकलना
न शम्भोस्तन्मूलं तव जननि ताटङ्क महिमा ॥

Sudhāmapyāsvādya Prati Bhaya Jarāmṛtyu Hariṇīṃ
Vipadyantē Viśvē Vidhi Śatamakhādyā Diviṣadaḥ |
Karālaṃ Yat Kṣvēlaṃ Kabalitavataḥ Kālakalanā
Na Śambhōstanmūlaṃ Tava Janani Tāṭaṅka Mahimā ||

The idea that **She** is the *Jeeva nāḍi* (soul pulse) of *Parameshwara* is being conveyed. Oh, mother mine, Gods like Indra and Brahma, who have drunk deep the nectar divine, which removes the cruel aging and death, do die and disappear. But Shambu thy consort, who swallowed poison that is potent, does never die, because of the greatness, of thine ear studs.

Śree Āchārya, describes with awe that *Śree Parameshwarā* could survive, even after consuming the *Halāhala* (poison), only by the power of *Śreedevee*'s *Tāṭankas.* That is the reason, *Sumangalees* are supposed to be always wearing the ear rings.

Even after consuming the great venom *Shiva* continued to live, on the other hand, even after consuming nectar, *Devas* get destroyed (during dissolution). Oh Mother! Gods lIke Indra and Brahma, who have drunk deep the nectar divine, which removes the cruel aging and death, do die and disappear. But Shambu thy consort, who swallowed poison that is potent, does never die, because of the greatness, of thine ear studs.

In *Lalita Sahasranama* 22ⁿᵈ Name –**Tāṭanka Yugaleebhoota Tapanodupa Maṇḍalā** – One who wears the Sun and Moon as two large earrings. One type of ornament worn by ladies in their ears is called *Tāṭanka* (palm leaf). The Sun and the Moon take the form of these *Tāṭankas* to beautify *Lalita*'s face. The Sun and the Moon have the fortune to become *Śreedevee*'s eyes, earrings and **Her** breasts. *Tāṭanka* is considered to be an auspicious ornament for *Sumangalees* (married ladies living with their husbands).

Again, in *Lalita Sahasranama* 373ʳᵈ Name – **Kāmeshvaraprāṇanāḍee** – One who is very life of **Her** consort *Kāmeshvara.* During the complete destruction of the universe (during the *pralaya* period), *devas* will also be destroyed, even if they have earlier consumed the nectar. But on the other hand, *Parameshwara,* who has consumed the most tyrant venom, is not destroyed – due to the grandeur of the earrings of *Śreedevee.*

The same sense is communicated in *Śree Rudram* also;

Ya Te Rudra Shivā Tanooḥ Shivā Vishvā Ha Bheshajee
Shiva Rudrasya Bheshajee Tayā No Mruḍa Jeevase ǀ

Verse #	28
Yantra with *Beeja* Letters	
Yantra Metal	Gold plate
Japa count #	1,000
# of Days	45
Daily offering	Milk payasam
Result	To get rid of all fears relating to poison

*****

29. किरीटं वैरिञ्चं परिहर पुरः कैटभभिदः
कठोरे कोटीरे स्कलसि जहि जम्भारि मकुटम् ।
प्रणम्रेष्वेतेषु प्रसभ मुपयातस्य भवनं
भवस्याभ्युत्थाने तव परिजनोक्ति र्विजयते ॥

Kirīṭaṃ Vairiñchaṃ Parihara Puraḥ Kaiṭabhabhidaḥ
Kaṭhōrē Kōṭīrē Skalasi Jahi Jambhāri Makuṭam ǀ
Praṇamrēṣvētēṣu Prasabha Mupayātasya Bhavanaṃ
Bhavasyābhyutthānē Tava Parijanōkti Rvijayatē ॥

Yours escorts divine, shout with concern at thee. "Avoid the crown of Brahma,
you may hit your feet, at the hard crown of Vishnu, who killed the ogre Kaidaba,
avoid the crown of Indra", when you get up and rush in a hurry,
to receive thine lord who comes to your place.

Verse #	29
Yantra with *Beeja* Letters	

Yantra Metal	Gold plate
Japa count #	1,000
# of Days	45
Daily offering	Sugar Pongal
Result	Attracting evil people

*****

30. स्वदेहोद्भूताभि घृणिभि रणिमाद्याभि रभितो
निषेव्ये नित्ये त्वा महमिति सदा भावयति यः ।
किमाश्चर्यं तस्य त्रिनयन समृद्धिं तृणयतो
महासंवर्ताग्नि विरचयति नीराजनविधिम् ॥

Svadēhōdbhūtābhi Rghṛnibhi Raṇimādyābhi Rabhitō
Niṣēvyē Nityē Tvā Mahamiti Sadā Bhāvayati Yaḥ I
Kimāścharyaṃ Tasya Trinayana Samṛddhiṃ Tṛṇayatō
Mahāsaṃvartāgni Rvirachayati Nīrājanavidhiṃ II

It is not surprising to know, Oh! Mother, who does not have birth and death, and who is most suitable to be served, that the destroying fire of the deluge, shows prayerful *hārathi* to the one, who considers you, (who is of the form of rays, and is surrounded on all four sides, by the angels of power called *Aṇimā*,) as his soul always, and who considers the wealth of the three eyed God, as worthless and as equal to dried grass.

In *Lalita Sahasranama* 393rd Name – **Prabhāvatee** – One who is endowed with the power of effulgence (luminescence). *Prabhā*, the surrounding *Āvaraṇadevatās*, namely *Aṇimā*, etc., because there is a saying, *Śreedevee* is surrounded by *aṇimā* and other luminaries. They originated as radiating light from the body of *Śreedevee*. In the *dyānā* (meditation) verse of this *Sahasranāma* also we read as; *Aṇimādibhirāvrutām Mayookhaiḥ*.

Verse #	30
Yantra with *Beeja* Letters	ॐ

Yantra Metal	Gold plate
Japa count #	1,000
# of Days	96
Daily offering	Three sweet items, Sugar Pongal, Honey, betel leaves
Result	Boldness, to enter others' body.

*****

31. चतुः षष्ट्या तन्त्रैः सकल मतिसन्धाय भुवनं
स्थितस्तत्त सिद्धि प्रसव परतन्त्रैः पशुपतिः ।
पुनस्त्व न्निर्बन्धा दखिल पुरुषार्थैक घटना
स्वतन्त्रं ते तन्त्रं क्षितितल मवातीतरदिदम् ॥

Chatuḥ Ṣaṣṭayā Tantraiḥ Sakala Matisandhāya Bhuvanaṃ
Sthitastattta Siddhi Prasava Paratantraiḥ Paśupatiḥ ।
Punastva Nnirbandhā Dakhila Puruṣārthaika Ghaṭanā
Svatantraṃ Tē Tantraṃ Kṣititala Mavātītaradidam ॥

This verse, says, thus *Shiva* originated 64 *tantras* to bewilder the common people. By the compulsion of *Śreedevee* he also made the 65th*tantra*, which explains the truth.

The Lord of all souls, Pasupathi, did create the sixty four *tantras*, each leading to only one desired power, and started his relaxation. But you goaded him mother, to create in this mortal world. Your *tantra* called *Srividya*, which grants the devotee, all powers that give powers, over all the states in life.

In *Lalita Sahasranama* 226th Name – **Mahātantra** – One who is the greatest *Tantra,* which conveys the method of worshipping **Herself**. The methods of worshipping and the books which explain them are called *Tantras*. They are *Kulārnavā, Jnānārnavā* and others. Since each of these is all great by itself, **she** is *Mahātantra*. When compared to other *Tantras, Swatantra,* explains the method of worshipping *Śreedevee* exclusively. It is a *Mahātantra*. Since **She** is worshipped with *Mahatantra* method, **she** is also *Mahātantra*. Lord *Parameshwarā* showed 64 *Tantras*. These are about various reigning deities giving various results. *Śreedevee* asked *Parameshwarā* to tell **Her** a *Tantra* which is greater than all these, which is complete and independent of itself. Then he explained a *Mahātantra* called *Swatantra*. This *Swatantra* is also called as *Rāja Tantra*.

Again, in *Lalita Sahasranama* 372nd Name – **Bhakta Mānasahamsikā** – One who is in the form of a swan in the lake like minds of the devotees. The creator, Brahma created a lake, by his mind. It is in the top of mount *Kailash*. Its water is so pure. The swans, which always like purity, live there in an infinite number. It has been described that wherever they travel, during rainy season return to this lake. It has been said in this name as – imaging the pure minds of the devotees to this lake (since it was created by mind, it is called *Mānasa Sarovar* (*Manas* – mind, *Sarovar* – lake) and *Śreedevee* compared to the swans living there.

She is invisible for others, that is, those other than devotees, mount, *ka* is suffixed and mentioned as *Hamsika*.

Again, in *Lalita Sahasranama* 703rd Name – **Sarvamohinee** – One who is all bewildering. How can this *Śreedevee* be said to possess contradictory attributes such as, permanence and impermanence, animation and non animation, etc. **She** bewilders all the ordinary people, who believe in the reality of the apparent duality; that is, **she** makes them devoid of the knowledge of unity. The meaning is that the apparent difference between *Brahmam* and the universe is illusory. In *Saptashatee* (I chapter) also it is mentioned as;

Gnānināmapi Chetamsi Devee Bhagavadee Hi Sā |
Balatākrushya Mohāya Mahāmāyā Prayachchati ||

In the *Koorma Purana*, *Shiva* says, "This supreme *Shakti* is in me and is *Brahmam* itself. This *Maya* is dear to me, infinite, by which this world is bewildered. Oh! best of the twice born ones, I bewilder the whole universe with the *Devas*, demons and men, and I create them and I cause them to exist";

In another place in the same *purana*, *Śreedevee* says to *Himavat*, "Whatever different scriptures are found in the world, opposed to *Shruti* and *Smriti*, devoted to the position of duality, namely *Kāpāla, Bhairava, Sakala, Gautama* and many similar ones, they are for the purpose of bewilderment; those who are confused by the false scriptures, also confuse the world, in another cycle; these were all created by me for the sake of bewilderment";

She bewilders *moha* the three worlds *sarva*, or this means **She** is in the form of *Trailokyamohanacakra* in *Śree chakra* and in the form of *Vidya*.

Again, in *Lalita Sahasranama* 723rd Name – **Svatantra** – One who acts on **Her** own without the help of others. **She** does not expect others' help for doing any activity. **She** does not even need any tool. By declaration itself, **she** does the acts. **She** owns **Her** consort *Parameshwara*. He owns **Her**. Mutually they own each other.

She has all the *tantras* as **Her** own *tantras*. The *Shaiva, Vaishnava* and *Gānapatya tantras* describe *Śreedevee*'s pride and hence can be considered as **Hers**. *Ganapati* and other gods can be worshipped only after installing (doing *Prāṇaprathishta*) them in the concerned idol or *yantra*. That *Prana* energy is *Śreedevee* only. Only with **Her** help the worship of other gods can be made. One commentator has explained that since the *tantras*, for which presiding deities are other gods, are also **Her** own, **she** is *Svatantra*.

She is in the form of *Nitya tantra* called *Svatantram*.

Again, in *Lalita Sahasranama* 945th Name – **Vāmakeshvaree** – One who is in the form of *Vamakeshvaratantra*. This *tantra* is about *Śree Devee*. In this in the part called *Nityāshoḍashikārnava*, lot of important matters about *Śree Devee* (its importance and meanings), the method of worshipping her, etc., have been described.

Those who follow the left path are called *Vāmakās*. They do not perform the five sacrifices viz., *Panchayajnās*. They do not repay the credits to *Devas*, sages (*rishis*) and *pitrus* (ancestors). **She** is head of them – i.e. **She** is worshipped by them.

Vamana indicates creation. *Daksha* and other *Prajapatis* who create the world are called *Vāmakās*. **She** is head of them.

Verse #	31
Yantra with *Beeja* Letters – (A little modified Sri Chakram):	
Yantra Metal	Gold plate
Japa count #	1,000
# of Days	45
Daily offering	Honey, Milk, Fruits

Result	Attract everything, to get every kind of wealth

*****

32. शिवः शक्तिः कामः क्षिति रथ रविः शीतकिरणः

स्मरो हंसः शक्र स्तदनु च परा मार हरयः ।

अमी हल्लेखाभि स्तिसृभि रवसानेषु घटिताः

भजन्ते वर्णास्ते तव जननि नामावयवताम् ॥

Śivaḥ Śaktiḥ Kāmaḥ Kṣiti Ratha Raviḥ Śītakiraṇaḥ
Smarō Haṃsaḥ Śakra Stadanu Cha Parā Māra Harayaḥ I
Amī Hṛllēkhābhi Stisṛbhi Ravasānēṣu Ghaṭitāḥ
Bhajantē Varṇāstē Tava Janani Nāmāvayavatām II

The commentary of *Śree Lakshmeedhara* this verse – She who is mother of us all. The seed letters of her *vidya* –

- The seed letter '*ka*' of my lord *Shiva*,
- The seed letter '*a*' of goddess *Shakti*,
- The seed letter '*ee*' of the god of love,
- The seed letter '*la*' of earth,
- The seed letter '*ha*' of the Sun god,
- The seed letter '*sa*' of the Moon with cool rays,
- The seed letter '*ka*' of again the god of love,
- The seed letter '*ha*' of the ether,
- The seed letter '*la*' of *Indra*, the king of *devas*,
- The seed letter '*sa*' of *Para*,
- The seed letter '*ka*' of the God of love,
- The seed letter '*la*' of the Lord *Vishnu*,

Along with your seed letters '*Hreem*', which joins at the end of each of the three holy wheels, become the holy word to worship you.

This gives indirectly the most holy *Panchadashākshari mantra*, which consists of three parts viz., *ka ā ee la hreem* at the end of *Vāgbhava koota*, *ha sa ka ha la hreem* at the end of *kamarāja koota* and *sa ka la hreem* at the end of *Shakti koota*.

These parts are respectively called *Vahni kundalini, Soorya Kundalini* and *Soma kundalini.*

In *Lalita Sahasranama* 391st Name – **Nityāshoḍashikāroopā** – We have presiding deities for the 15 days from first to full Moon day. They are all the limbs of *Śreedevee. Śreedevee* herself is the sixteenth *nityā* – i.e., *Mahānitya.* **She** is also called as *Sādākya Kala.*

Verse #	32
Yantra with *Beeja* Letters	
Yantra Metal	Gold plate – to tie the plate in the place of business
Japa count #	1,000
# of Days	45
Daily offering	Curd rice, Black gram vadai, Sugar Pongal
Result	Success in business

*****

33. स्मरं योनिं लक्ष्मीं त्रितय मिद मादौ तव मनो
निधायैके नित्ये निरवधि महाभोग रसिकाः ।
भजन्ति त्वां चिन्तामणि गुणनिबद्धाक्ष वलयाः
शिवाग्नौ जुह्वन्तः सुरभिघृत धाराहुति शतै ॥

Smaraṃ Yōniṃ Lakṣmīṃ Tritaya Mida Mādau Tava Manō
Rnidhāyaikē Nityē Niravadhi Mahābhōga Rasikāḥ I
Bhajanti Tvāṃ Chintāmaṇi Guṇanibaddhākṣa Valayāḥ
Śivāgnau Juhvantaḥ Surabhighṛta Dhārāhuti Śatai II

Oh, mother who is ever present, those who realise the essence, of the limitless pleasure of the soul you give and who add the seed letter *'Kleem'* of the god of love, the seed letter *'Hreem'* of the goddess Bhuavaneswaree, and the seed letter *'Shreem'* of the goddess Lakshmi, which are the three letter triad, wear the garland of the gem of thoughts and offer oblations to the fire in triangle of *Sri Chakra*, with the pure scented ghee of the holy cow, Kamadhenu, several times and worship you.

Verse #	33
Yantra with *Beeja* Letters	श्री
Yantra Metal	Gold plate – to keep money in closed hand and to perform the japam
Japa count #	1,000
# of Days	45
Daily offering	Honey, mixed rice
Result	Economic development in life

*****

34. शरीरं त्वं शम्भोः शशि मिहिर वक्षोरुह युगं
तवात्मानं मन्ये भगवति नवात्मान मनघम् ।
अतः शेषः शेषीत्यय मुभय साधारणतया
स्थितः सम्बन्धो वां समरस परानन्द परयोः ॥

Śarīraṃ Tvaṃ Śambhōḥ Śaśi Mihira Vakṣōruha Yugaṃ
Tavātmānaṃ Manyē Bhagavati Navātmāna Managham ǀ
Ataḥ Śēṣaḥ Śēṣītyaya Mubhaya Sādhāraṇatayā
Sthitaḥ Sambandhō Vāṃ Samarasa Parānanda Parayōḥ ǀǀ

The commentaries mention that there are five different characteristics for *Shiva Shakti*. They are;

a.   Equality in worshipping with *chakra*, etc., – *Atishṭāna Sāmyam* (quality in installation)
b.   Equality in tasks like creation, protection, etc., – *Anushtānā Sāmyam* (quality of tasks)
c.   Equality in actions like dance, etc., – *Avastāna Sāmyam* (quality of actions)
d.   Equality in names like *Shivā Shiva, Bhairavee Bhairava*, etc., – *Nāma Sāmyam*

(quality of names)

e. Equality in Red colour (this has originated from white), three eyes, crescent Moon, etc., – *Roopa Sāmyam* (quality of form)

In *Śree Chakra*, **her** form is the union of *Shiva Chakra* and *Shakti Chakra*. In *Śree Chakra* the upward four *chakras* are *Shiva Chakras* and downward five *chakras* are *Shakti Chakras*.

In *Lalita Sahasranama* 999th Name – ***Shivashaktyaikyaroopiṇee*** – One who is the unison of *Shiva* and *Shakti*. **She** embodies the union of *Shiva* and *Shakti*. **She** is the universal absolute and cannot be considered as individual *Shiva* or *Shakti* forms – must be considered in the integrated unison form.

Here 'union' means the supreme equality, the being of absolute unity without any differences. The *Saura Samhita* says, "The *Shakti*, which is separate from *Brahmam* is not different from *Brahmam* itself. Such being the case it is only called *Shakti* (as separate) by the ignorant. It is impossible to distinguish the difference, between the *Shakti* and the possessor of *Shakti*".

Verse #	34
Yantra with *Beeja* Letters	
Yantra Metal	Gold plate
Japa count #	1,000
# of Days	45
Daily offering	Pepper powder with ghee
Result	To get rid off all water related diseases

*****

35. मनस्त्वं व्योम त्वं मरुदसि मरुत्सारथि रसि

त्वमाप स्त्वं भूमि स्त्वयि परिणतायां न हि परम् ।

त्वमेव स्वात्मानं परिणमयितुं विश्व वपुषा

चिदानन्दाकारं शिवयुवति भावेन बिभृषे ॥

Manastvam Vyōma Tvaṃ Marudasi Marutsārathi Rasi

Tvamāpa Stvaṃ Bhūmi Stvayi Pariṇatāyāṃ Na Hi Param |
Tvamēva Svātmānaṃ Pariṇamayituṃ Viśva Vapuṣā
Chidānandākāraṃ Śivayuvati Bhāvēna Bibhṛṣē ||

Oh, goddess supreme, I always see in my internal eyes, that your body with Sun and Moon, as busts is the body of Shiva, and his peerless body with nine surrounding motes, is your body, my mother. And so, the relation of, "that which has", and "he who has", becomes the one perfect relation of happiness and becomes equal in each of you.

The philosophies relating to mind you are, Ether you are, Air you are, Fire you are, Water you are, Earth you are and you are the universe, my Mother! There is nothing accept you in the world, but to make believe your form as the universe, you take the role of consort of Lord Shiva and appear before us in the form of ethereal happiness.

Verse #	35
Yantra with *Beeja* Letters	
Yantra Metal	Gold plate
Japa count #	1,000
# of Days	45
Daily offering	Sugar, honey, payasam
Result	To get rid off leprosy diseases

*****

36. तवाज्ञचक्रस्थं तपन शशि कोटि द्युतिधरं
परं शंभुं वन्दे परिमिलित पार्श्व परचिता ।
यमाराध्यन् भक्त्या रवि शशि शुचीना मविषये
निरालोके ऽलोके निवसति हि भालोक भुवने ॥

Tavājjñachakrastham Tapana Śaśi Kōṭi Dyutidharaṃ
Param Śambhum Vandē Parimilita Pārśvam Parachitā |
Yamārādhyan Bhaktyā Ravi Śaśi Suchīnā Maviṣayē

Nirālōkē 'Lōkē Nivasati Hi Bhālōka Bhuvanē ॥

The details of these *Guṇas/ Vyoohas* are given in the commentary of *Lakshmeedhara*. The one who worships Parameshwara, who has the luster of billions of Moon and Sun and who lives in thine *Agna chakra* the holy wheel of order, and is surrounded by thine two forms, on both sides, would forever live, in that world where rays of Sun and Moon do not enter, but which has its own luster, and which is beyond the sight of the eye, but is different from the world seen.

In *Lalita Sahasranama* 103rd Name – **Āgyāchakrantarālasthā** – *Āgyā Chakra* reposes between the two eye brows, in the *Sushumnanāḍi* with two petals. It is the place of the teacher who gives orders (*Āgyā*): Hence *Āgyā Chakra*. On account of practice done so far, the mind is controlled a little (*Ā* also means very little) and knowledge is acquired, this is called *Āgyā Chakra*.

Again in *Lalita Sahasranama* 521st Name – **Āgnāchakrabjanilayā** – One who resides in the *Āgnā chakra* Lotus – in between the eye brows.

Again in *Lalita Sahasranama* 604th Name – **Guṇanidhiḥ** – One who is the treasure house of qualities. The *Sānkhya* doctrine says that though the qualities are specifically three viz. *sattva*, *rajas* and *tamas*, they have endless modifications. **She** is the treasure house of all such qualities.

Guṇa means aggregate (*Vyoohas*). Like nine *nidhies*, these *vyoohas* also are nine in number. *Parameshwara* is of the form of these nine aggregates of qualities. They are; *Kālavyooha* (time), *Kulavyooha* (family race), *Nāmavyooha* (name), *Gnānavyooha* (knowledge), *Chittavyooha* (mind), *Nadavyooha* (*Nātha*), *Binduvyooha* (*Bindu*), *Kalpavyooha* (*Kalpa*) and *Jeevavyooha* (soul). Since **She** is of these forms **She** is called as *Guṇanidhi*.

The word *Guṇa* also means rope. The rope called *Valrikā*, which tied the ship during the *pralaya*; *Nidhi*, the deity to whom it was tied. The following story occurs in the *Matsya* and *Kālika Puranas* thus; at the time of dissolution all seeds and sages entered the boat at the command of *Manu*, who was directed by the Lord *Vishnu*, and the boat was tied to the horn of the fish incarnation. That rope became firm when *Śreedevee* held it. "Make a great rope of hides to be called *Vatrikā*, nine *Yojanas* long and three cubits broad. *Śreedevee* who is the protector of the universe, the great *Maya*, the mother of the world, the world itself, will make that rope firm so that it will not give away".

The one who worships Parameshwara, who has the luster of billions of Moon and Sun and who lives in thine Agna chakra – the holy wheel of order and is surrounded by thine two forms (both *saguna* and *nirguna*), on both sides, would forever live, in that world where rays of sun and moon do not enter, but which has its own luster and which is beyond the sight of the eye, but is different from the world we see.

Verse #	36
Yantra with *Beeja* Letters	ठ य श ढं ढं ढं
Yantra Metal	Gold plate – the verse and the chakra can be written in water in a cup and take bath after japam.
Japa count #	1,000
# of Days	45
Daily offering	Vadai, Athirasam, payasam
Result	To get rid off all types of diseases

*****

37. विशुद्धौ ते शुद्धस्फटिक विशदं व्योम जनकं
शिवं सेवे देवीमपि शिवसमान व्यवसिताम् ।
ययो: कांत्या यांत्या: शशिकिरण् सारूप्यसरणे:
विधूतान्त ध्वान्ता विलसति चकोरीव जगती ॥

Viśuddhau Tē Śuddhasphaṭika Viśadaṃ Vyōma Janakaṃ
Śivaṃ Sēvē Dēvīmapi Śivasamāna Vyavasitām I
Yayōḥ Kāntyā Yāntyāḥ Śaśikiraṇ Sārūpyasaraṇēḥ
Vidhūtānta Rdhvāntā Vilasati Chakōrīva Jagatī II

I bow before Shiva, who is of the pure crystal form, in thine supremely pure *vishuddhi chakra* and who creates the principle of ether and to you my mother, who has same stream of thought as Him. I bow before you both, whose Moon like light, forever removes the darkness of ignorance, forever from the mind and which shines like the Chakora bird, playing in the full Moon light.

In *Lalita Sahasranama* 475th Name – **Vishuddhichakra Nilayā** – One who abodes in the *Vishuddhi Chakra*.

This *chakra* is in the cavity of the throat. In this *chakra*, the soul gets purified by looking at the *Brahmam*, in the form of a swan. Hence this is called as *Vishuddhi Chakra*. **Her** abode is in the pericarp of the sixteen petalled lotus.

Verse #	37
Yantra with *Beeja* Letters	
Yantra Metal	Gold plate.
Japa count #	5,000
# of Days	45
Daily offering	Vadai, payasam, coconut, fruits
Result	To get rid off all types of evils.

*****

38. समुन्मीलत् संवित्कमल मकरन्दैक रसिकं
भजे हंसद्वन्द्वं किमपि महतां मानसचरम् ।
यदालापात् अष्टादश गुणित विद्यापरिणतिः
यदादत्ते दोषात् गुण मखिल मद्भ्यः पय इव ॥

Samunmīlat Saṃvitkamala Makarandaika Rasikaṃ
Bhajē Haṃsadvandvaṃ Kimapi Mahatāṃ Mānasacharaṃ I
Yadālāpāt Aṣṭādaśa Guṇita Vidyāpariṇatiḥ
Yadādattē Dōṣāt Guṇa Makhila Madbhyaḥ Paya Iva II

I pray before the swan couple, who only enjoy the honey, from the fully open, Lotus flowers of knowledge, and who swim in the lake, which is the mind of great ones, and also who can never be described. From them come the eighteen arts, and they differentiate the good from the bad, like the milk from water.
In *Lalita Sahasranama* 372nd Name – **Bhakta Mānasahamsikā** – One who is in the form of a swan in the lake like minds of the devotees. The creator, Brahma created a lake, by his mind. It is in the top of mount *Kailash*. Its water is so pure.

The swans, which always like purity, live there in an infinite number. It has been described that wherever they travel, during rainy season return to this lake. It has been said in this name as – imaging the pure minds of the devotees to this lake (since it was created by mind, it is called *Mānasa Sarovar* (*Manas* – mind, *Sarovar* – lake) and *Śreedevee* compared to the swans living there.

I pray before the swan couple, who only enjoy the honey, from the fully open, lotus flowers of knowledge and who swim in the lake, which is the mind of great ones and also who can never be described. From them come the 18 arts and they differentiate the good from the bad, like the milk from water.

Again in *Lalita Sahasranama* 485th Name – **Anāhatābjanilayā** – One who abodes in the *Anāhata* Lotus. This is in the heart with twelve petalled lotus. This is the place of air.

Verse #	38
Yantra with *Beeja* Letters	कं
Yantra Metal	Gold plate.
Japa count #	5,000
# of Days	45
Daily offering	Any offering
Result	To get rid off all types of evils.

*****

39. तव स्वाधिष्ठाने हुतवह मधिष्ठाय निरतं
तमीडे संवर्त जननि महतीं तां च समयाम् ।
यदालोके लोकान् दहति महसि क्रोध कलिते
दयार्द्रा या दृष्टिः शिशिर मुपचारं रचयति ॥

Tava Svādhiṣṭhānē Hutavaha Madhiṣṭhāya Niratam
Tamīḍē Saṃvartam Janani Mahatīm Tām Cha Samayām ।
Yadālōkē Lōkān Dahati Mahasi Krōdha Kalitē
Dayārdrā Yā Dṛṣṭiḥ Śiśira Mupachāram Rachayati ॥

Oh Mother! I think and worship, of the fire, in your holy wheel of Swadishtana and Sri Rudra who shines in that fire, like the destroying fire of deluge and you who shine there as Samaya. When that angry fire of look of Rudra, burns the world, then your look drenches it in mercy, which treats and cools it down.

In *Lalita Sahasranama* 504th Name – ***Svādhishṭānāmbujagatā*** – One who abodes in the *Svādhishṭāna chakra* (in the lower abdomen of the body). *Svādhishṭāna* is the place of water. Hence starting from ether until water the four primary elements represent the four faces of *Śreedevee*. The 14th verse of *Soundaryalaharee* can also be referred, which states *Svādhishṭāna* as the place of fire and *Maṇipooraka* as the place of water.

Verse #	39
Yantra with *Beeja* Letters	ठं पं प: षं सं
Yantra Metal	Gold plate.
Japa count #	108
# of Days	12
Daily offering	Pongal, Milk payasam, honey
Result	To get rid off bad dreams.

*****

40. तटित्वन्तं शक्त्या तिमिर परिपन्थि स्फुरणया
स्फुर न्ना नारत्नाभरण परिणद्धेन्द्र धनुषम् ।
तव श्यामं मेघं कमपि मणिपूरैक शरणं
निषेवे वर्षन्तं हरमिहिर तप्तं त्रिभुवनम् ॥

Taṭitvantaṃ Śaktyā Timira Paripanthi Sphuraṇayā
Sphura Nnā Nāratnābharaṇa Pariṇaddhēndra Dhanuṣam ǀ
Tava Śyāmaṃ Mēghaṃ Kamapi Maṇipūraika Śaraṇaṃ
Niṣēvē Varṣantaṃ Haramihira Taptaṃ Tribhuvanam ǁ
I bow before that principle, which is in your wheel of *Manipooraka*, which as *Parashakthi* shines like the enemy of darkness, which is with the streak of lightning, which is with the shining jewels of precious stones of lightning, which

is also black as night, which is burnt by Rudra like the Sun of the deluge and which cools down the three worlds like a strange cloud.

In *Lalita Sahasranama* 101st Name – **Maṇipoorāntaruditā** – The lotus with ten petals near the belly button is called *maṇipooram*. This is also named as *Sthithi Chakra*, place of *Viṣhṇu* and *Soorya Kaṇḍam*. *Śree Devee* is decorated with various gems (*Maṇis*) and hence *Maṇipoorakam*.

Again in *Lalita Sahasranama* 495th Name – **Maṇipoorābjanilayā** – One who resides in the lotus called *Maṇipoora*. It is in the belly button with 10 petals.

Verse #	40
Yantra with *Beeja* Letters	
Yantra Metal	Gold plate – to keep beneath the pillow while sleeping
Japa count #	1,000
# of Days	45
Daily offering	Milk, payasam, betel leaves
Result	To get dreams of choice.

*****

41. तवाधारे मूले सह समयया लास्यपरया
नवात्मानं मन्ये नवरस महाताण्डव नटम् ।
उभाभ्या मेताभ्या मुदय विधि मुद्दिश्य दयया
सनाथाभ्यां जज्ञे जनक जननीमज्जगदिदम् ॥

Tavādhārē Mūlē Saha Samayayā Lāsyaparayā
Navātmānam Manyē Navarasa Mahātāṇḍava Naṭam l

Ubhābhyā Mētābhyā Mudaya Vidhi Muddiśya Dayayā
Sanāthābhyāṃ Jajjṇē Janaka Jananīmajjagadidam ll

The dance of Lord *Shiva* and Goddess *Shakti* has been compared in this verse.

I pray in your holy wheel of *Moolādhāra*, you who like to dance, and calls yourself as *Samaya*, and that Lord who performs the great vigorous dance, which has all the shades of nine emotions. This world has you both as parents, because you in your mercy, wed one another, to recreate the world, as the world was destroyed in the grand deluge.

In *Lalita Sahasranama* 232nd Name – **Maheshvara Mahākalpa Mahātāṇḍava Sākshiṇee** – One who is the witness to the great awesome destructive cosmic dance of Lord *Maheshvarā* at the end of creative cycle. *Mahākalpa* means the great dissolution (*pralaya*) of this universe; destruction means – the entire universe sub merged with Lord himself. This is the fourth task of *Śreedevee* called *Thirodhāna*. Lord *Maheshvara* was pleased by sub merging within him all that was created. On account of this he gives a visual treat in the form of a dance called *Mahātāndava*. At this time *Śreedevee* was the only remaining witness to this dance. **She** is the only witness right before creation till complete destruction. The dance by men is called *tāndavā* and that of women is *lāsya.* It has been mentioned that when *Maheshvara* did the *Tāndavā*, *Śreedevee* also did the *Lāsya.* When both are dancing, at the request of *Śreedevee*, both started the fifth task called *Anugrahā* by re creating the entire universe with most compassion.

Again in *Lalita Sahasranama* 99th Name – **Moolādhāraikanilayā** – One whose main residence is *Moolādhāram*. The backbone of the body is called *Merudhaṇḍam*. The *nāḍi* called *Sushumna* runs inside this. The bottom most part of this is the butt. In the midst of this, the *Linga* stays in a place called *Moolādhāram*. *Moolādhāra* Lotus has four petals. *Kuṇḍalinee* always sleeps, keeping it head downwards, in the *bindu* called *Kulakuṇḍam*, in a *karnika* in this *chakra*. Hence it is said as *Śreedevee*, in the form of *Kuṇḍalinee*, has *Moolādhāra* as **Her** main dwelling. It is called *Moolādhāra*, since it is the base for *Kuṇḍalinee* and also the root of *Sushumna*.

Again in *Lalita Sahasranama* 514th Name – **Moolādhārāmbujāroodhā** – One who dwells in *Moolādhāra* Lotus. *Moolādhāra* is the lower abdomen in the body. **She** resides in the Lotus in that place. *Moolādhāra* is the place of earth *tatva*. Hence **She** has five faces indicating the five primary elements ether till earth.

In *Gaṇapati Atharva Seersha Upanishat* also it is mentioned – *Tvam Moolādhārastoṣsi Nityam* – you (Lord *Gaṇapati*) reside permanently in *Moolādhāram*.

Again, in *Lalita Sahasranama* 734th Name – **Naṭeshvaree** – One who is the consort of *Naṭesha*. This means that **She** is the consort of *Nataraja*, dancing in *Chidambaram*. The word *Chidambara* can be taken in two meanings – the place *Chidambara* or the ether of heart. Both are befitting meanings. **She** dances alongwith *Natesa*.

Again, in *Lalita Sahasranama* 738th Name – **Lāsyapriyā** – One who is fond of dancing. The dance performed by women is called *lāsya* (whereas male's dance is called *tāndava*).

She is pleased by seeing dance of others. In general, ordinary people also are pleased with songs and dance. It has been practiced for long wherein artists perform in front of kings and get rewarded. In the court of the empress *Śreedevee* also dance and music performances are given. It is clear that these performances are made in temples also.

A king, who has got satisfied with all his desires, without attaining any fruits, enjoys hunting, games of children, etc. In the same way *Śreedevee* also enjoys the dance showing four fold desirable, undesirable, mixed and abuse and the resultant happiness and sorrow and the consequent facial expressions, the shaking of legs, hands and other organs. Thus, enjoyed *Śreedevee* bestows the results of the actions of devotees without any partiality; *Nā Datte Kshyachipāpam Na Chaiva Sukrutam Vibhuḥ*. Or She is pleased with the dance according to the tune and drums performed by *Ramba, Urvashi* and other *Devata* ladies.

Note; Last six verses described the importance of worshipping *Sri Devi* in the form of *Shiva Shakti*, in each of six chakras in the human body. Also, each of five primary elements and the related philosophies are mapped.

Verse #	41
Yantra with *Beeja* Letters	यं ह्रीं
antra Metal	Gold plate – to keep the chakra in salt and the salt can be consumed after the japam
Japa count #	4,000
# of Days	30
Daily offering	Pongal
Result	To get rid off any stomach related diseases.

*****

द्वितीय भागः – *Dwitīya Bhāgaḥ – Second Part –* **सौन्दर्यलहरी** – *Soundaryalaharī*

The second part (verses 42 to 100) is entirely devoted to describe the beauty of *Śree Devee* only. This part describes the great mother Shakthi from head to foot.

In *Lalita Sahasranama* 972nd Name – **Āshobhanā** – One who is always and everywhere beautiful. The beauty of *Śree Devee* has been mentioned in many a place in the *Sahasranāma*.

In this part in almost all the places *Sri Adi Shankarar* addresses *Sri Devi* as "Daughter of Himavan Mountain" in different ways. Moreover, he calls *Ambika* singularly and with liberty as 'you' and 'your'. Other than a son who else can have a right and liberty with mother?

*****

42. गतै र्माणिक्यत्वं गगनमणिभिः सान्द्रघटितं
किरीटं ते हैमं हिमगिरिसुते कीर्तयति यः ॥
स नीडेयच्छाया च्छुरण शबलं चन्द्र शकलं
धनुः शौनासीरं किमिति न निबध्नाति धिषणाम् ॥

Gatai Rmāṇikyatvaṃ Gaganamaṇibhiḥ Sāndraghaṭitaṃ
Kirīṭaṃ Tē Haimaṃ Himagirisutē Kīrtayati Yaḥ ।
Sa Nīḍēyachchhāyā Chchuraṇa Śabalaṃ Chandra Śakalaṃ
Dhanuḥ Śaunāsīraṃ Kimiti Na Nibadhnāti Dhiṣaṇām ॥

Hey daughter of the ice mountain, he who chooses to describe, your crown, bedecked with shining jewels, which are but the transformed form and arranged very close to one another, of the twelve holy Suns, will see the crescent in your crown, in the dazzling light of those jewels and think them as a rainbow, which is but the bow of the Indra.

Verse #	42
Yantra with *Beeja* Letters	

Yantra Metal	Gold plate – to keep the chakra in till flour with Alwin and the same can be consumed after the japam
Japa count #	1,000
# of Days	45
Daily offering	Milk, sugar
Result	To get rid off any water related diseases.

*****

43. धुनोतु ध्वान्तं न स्तुलित दलितेन्दीवर वनं
घनस्निग्ध श्लक्ष्णं चिकुर निकुरुम्बं तव शिवे ।
यदीयं सौरभ्यं सहज मुपलब्धुं सुमनसो
वसन्त्यस्मिन् मन्ये वलमथन वाटी विटपिनाम् ॥

Dhunōtu Dhvāntaṃ Na Stulita Daḻitēndīvara Vanaṃ
Ghanasnigdha Ślakṣṇaṃ Chikura Nikurumbaṃ Tava Śivē |
Yadīyaṃ Saurabhyaṃ Sahaja Mupalabdhuṃ Sumanasō
Vasantyasmin Manyē Valamathana Vāṭī Viṭapinām ||

Oh, Goddess! the consort of Lord Shiva, let the darkness of our mind be destroyed, by the crowning glory on your head, which is of like the forest of opened blue lotus flowers and which is soft, dense and shines with luster. I believe my mother that the pretty flowers of Indra's Garden, are all forever there, to get the natural scent of thine hair.

The debate between the poet Nakkeera and Lord Shiva "whether the aroma of the hair of ladies is natural or artificial" can be connected in this context.

Verse #	43
Yantra with Beeja Letters	श्रीं
Yantra Metal	Gold plate – Gold ring
Japa count #	1,000

# of Days	45
Daily offering	Mixed rice
Result	To get rid off any disease. Success in all tasks

*****

44. तनोतु क्षेमं न स्तव वदनसौन्दर्यलहरी
परीवाहस्रोतः सरणिरिव सीमन्तसरणिः।
वहन्ती सिन्दूरं प्रबलकबरी भार तिमिर
द्विषां बृन्दै र्वन्दीकृतमिव नवीनार्क किरणम् ॥

Tanōtu Kṣēmaṃ Na Stava VadanaSoundaryalaharī
Parīvāhasrōtaḥ Saraṇiriva Sīmantasaraṇiḥ
Vahantī Sindūraṃ Prabalakabarī Bhāra Timira
Dviṣāṃ Bṛndai Rbandīkṛtamiva Navīnārka Kiraṇam ॥

Oh mother, let the line parting thine hairs, which looks like a canal, through which the rushing waves of your beauty ebbs and which on both sides imprisons, your Vermillion, which is like a rising Sun by using your hair which is dark like, the platoon of soldiers of the enemy, protect us and give us peace.

Verse #	44
Yantra with *Beeja* Letters	ह्रीं
Yantra Metal	Gold plate – Turmeric Kumkum
Japa count #	1,008
# of Days	12
Daily offering	Honey
Result	To get rid off any disease.

*****

45. अरालै स्वाभाव्या दलिकलभ सश्रीभि रलकैः
परीतं ते वक्त्रं परिहसति पङ्केरुहरुचिम् ।
दरस्मेरे यस्मिन् दशनरुचि किञ्जल्क रुचिरे
सुगन्धौ माद्यन्ति स्मरदहन चक्षु र्मधुलिहः ॥

Arālai Svābhāvyā Dalikalabha Saśrībhi Ralakaiḥ
Parītaṃ Tē Vaktraṃ Parihasati Paṅkēruharuchim ।
Darasmērē Yasmin Daśanaruchi Kiñjalka Ruchirē
Sugandhau Mādyanti Smaradahana Chakṣu Rmadhulihaḥ ॥

By nature, slightly curled, and shining like the young honey bees, your golden thread like hairs, surround your golden face. Your face makes fun of the beauty of the lotus. And adorned with slightly parted smile, showing the tiers of your teeth, which are like the white tendrils and which are sweetly scented. Bewitches the eyes of God, who burnt the god of love (Cupid).

Verse #	45
Yantra with *Beeja* Letters	
Yantra Metal	Gold plate
Japa count #	1,000
# of Days	45
Daily offering	Honey
Result	To improve speech

****

46. ललाटं लावण्य द्युति विमल माभाति तव यत्
द्वितीयं तन्मन्ये मकुटघटितं चन्द्रशकलम् ।
विपर्यास न्यासा दुभयमपि सम्भूय च मिथः
सुधालेपस्यूतिः परिणमति राका हिमकरः ॥

Lalāṭaṃ Lāvaṇya Dyuti Vimala Mābhāti Tava Yat
Dvitīyaṃ Tanmanyē Makuṭaghaṭitaṃ Chandraśakalam |
Viparyāsa Nyāsā Dubhayamapi Sambhūya Cha Mithaḥ
Sudhālēpasyūtiḥ Pariṇamati Rākā Himakaraḥ ||

Āchārya beautifully describes this as that the forehead as a half Moon is so beautiful and it complements the half Moon in the crown so that the circle of the Moon is complete.

I suspect Oh, mother! That your forehead, which shines with the beauty of the Moon, is but an imprisoned half moon, by your glorious crown, for if joined opposite to the inverted half moon in your crown, it would give out the nectar like luster, of the full Moon.

In *Lalita Sahasranama* 15th Name – **Ashṭameechandra Vibhrājadalikasthala Shobhitā** – One whose forehead shines like the Moon on the eighth day of lunar half month. Of the fifteen phases of the Moon, on the eighth day of bright lunar half month, the eighth phase will be seen. Or reduced upto eight phases on the eighth day of the lunar dark half month the Moon will be visible as a semicircle. In the emerging form of *Śreedevee* from the sacrificial fire, the crown, hair and flowers come out one after the other and the forehead emerges as an inverted semicircle resembling the eighth day Moon, with flawless cool light.

Verse #	46
Yantra with *Beeja* Letters	ह्रीं
Yantra Metal	Gold plate
Japa count #	1,000
# of Days	45
Daily offering	Honey, Milk, Payasam
Result	To get a child

*****

47. भ्रुवौ भुग्ने किञ्चिद्भुवन भय भङ्गव्यसनिनि
त्वदीये नेत्राभ्यां मधुकर रुचिभ्यां धृतगुणम् ।
धनु र्मन्ये सव्येतरकर गृहीतं रतिपतेः
प्रकोष्ठे मुष्टौ च स्थगयति निगूढान्तर मुमे ॥

Bhruvau Bhugnē Kiñchidbhuvana Bhaya Bhaṅgavyasanini
Tvadīyē Nētrābhyāṃ Madhukara Ruchibhyāṃ Dhṛtaguṇam I
Dhanu Rmanyē Savyētarakara Gṛhītaṃ Ratipatēḥ
Prakōṣṭē Muṣṭau Cha Sthagayati Nigūḍhāntara Mumē II

Oh! Goddess Uma, **she** who removes fear from the world, the slightly bent eye brows of yours, tied by a hoard of honey bees forming the string, I feel resembles the bow of the god of love held by his left hand and having hidden middle part, hid by the wrist, and folded fingers.

In *Lalita Sahasranama* 461st Name – **Subhrooḥ** – One who has beautiful eye brows.

Within the time taken for *Śreedevee*'s eye brows to bend up and come down, many four aeon would have completed. While detailing the period by *Ashṭānga* method it has been mentioned as; *Uurdhva Bhroo Vibhrame.*

Verse #	47
Yantra with *Beeja* Letters	
Yantra Metal	Gold plate or vibhooti. The plate should be kept on head during japam.
Japa count #	1,000
# of Days	25
Daily offering	Honey, fruits, coconut
Result	Success in all tasks

*****

48. अहः सूते सव्यं तव नयन मर्कात्मकतया
त्रियामां वामं ते सृजति रजनीनायकतया ।
तृतीया ते दृष्टि ददरदलित हेमाम्बुज रुचिः
समाधत्ते सन्ध्यां दिवसर् निशयो रन्तरचरीम् ॥

Ahaḥ Sūtē Savyam Tava Nayana Markātmakatayā
Triyāmām Vāmam Tē Sṛjati Rajanīnāyakatayā I
Tṛtīyā Tē Dṛṣṭi Rdaradalita Hēmāmbuja Ruchiḥ
Samādhattē Sandhyām Divasar Niśayō Rantaracharīm II

Right eye of yours is like the Sun and makes the day, left eye of yours is like the Moon and creates the night, thine middle eye, which is like the golden lotus bud, slightly opened into a flower, makes the dawn and the dusk.

Verse #	48
Yantra with *Beeja* Letters	<table><tr><td>बु</td><td>शु</td><td>च</td></tr><tr><td>गु</td><td>र</td><td>कु</td></tr><tr><td>रा</td><td>श</td><td>के</td></tr></table>
Yantra Metal	Gold plate.
Japa count #	1,000
# of Days	45
Daily offering	Honey, fruits, mixed rice
Result	To get rid off negative effects of the nine planets.

*****

49. विशाला कल्याणी स्फुटरुचि रयोध्या कुवलयैः
कृपाधाराधारा किमपि मधुराऽभोगवतिका ।
अवन्ती दृष्टिस्ते बहुनगर विस्तार विजया
ध्रुवं तत्तन्नाम व्यवहरण योग्याविजयते ॥

Viśālā Kalyāṇī Sphuṭaruchi Rayōdhyā Kuvalayaiḥ
Kṛpādhārādhārā Kimapi Madhurā"bhōgavatikā I

Avantī Dṛṣṭistē Bahunagara Vistāra Vijayā
Dhruvaṃ Tattannāma Vyavaharaṇa Yōgyāvijayatē ‖

Vishālā means blossomed sight. In commentaries this has been mentioned as energy that creates confusion. This verse stresses this angle.

The look from your eyes, Oh! Goddess is all pervasive, does good to everyone, sparkles everywhere, is a beauty that can never be challenged, even by blue lily flowers, is the source of rain of mercy, is sweetness personified, is long and pretty, is capable of saving devotees, is in the several cities as its victory and can be called by several names, according to which aspect one sees.

In *Lalita Sahasranama* 936th Name – **Vishālākshee** – One who has long and large eyes. The eyes leading upto the ears will be beautiful. According to *Padma Purana*, *Vishālākshee* is the name of the deity worshipped at *Banaras*. **She** is of that form.

The word *Vishālā* indicates *Badrikāshrama*. Since it is in the Himalayas, it also indicates *Nepala Peeṭa*. In *Laghu Shoḍa Nyāsa* (*Peeṭa Nyāsā*), *Brahmānḍa* and other *Puranas* say, that the *Nepala Peeṭa* should be meditated upon as situated in the eyes. The word *Akshee* indicates both the eyes. Hence it can be considered that **She** has *Vishāla Peeṭa* as her eyes.

Verse #	49
Yantra with *Beeja* Letters	मक्ल मक्ल मक्ल मक्ल (*yantra* diagram)
Yantra Metal	Gold plate. The yantra can be drawn in turmeric paste and heat the same. After japam it can be mixed with till oil and applied on the eyes.
Japa count #	1,000
# of Days	10
Daily offering	Honey, Pongal
Result	To get rid off eye diseases. To have the vision of Gods/ Goddesses.

*****

50. कवीनां सन्दर्भ स्तबक मकरन्दैक रसिकं
कटाक्ष व्याक्षेप भ्रमरकलभौ कर्णयुगलम् ।
अमुञ्च्न्तौ दृष्ट्वा तव नवरसास्वाद तरलौ
असूया संसर्गा तलिकनयनं किञ्चिदरुणम् ॥

Kavīnāṃ Sandarbha Stabaka Makarandaika Rasikaṃ
Kaṭākṣa Vyākṣēpa Bhramarakalabhau Karṇayugalam |
Amuñchntau Dṛṣṭvā Tava Navarasāsvāda Taralau
Asūyā Saṃsargā Talikanayanaṃ Kiñchidaruṇam ||

Lot many verses of this text, importantly this verse, 52 and 57th verses, describe the beauty and the glory of the eyes of Sri Devi.

Thine two long eyes, Oh! Goddess, are like the two little bees, which want to drink the honey, and extend to the ends with a pretense of side glances, to thine two ears, which are bent upon drinking the honey, from the flower bunch of poems, presented by your devotees, and make thine third eye light purple, with jealousy and envy.

In *Lalita Sahasranama* 601st Name – **Darāndolitadeerghākshee** – One who has wavering wide eyes extending upto her ears. *Darā* means a little/ slightly. The eyes of *Śreedevee* slightly waver on all sides. The eyes of *Śreedevee* are extended upto her ears. As per the characters declared in physiognomy the eyes extending upto the ears are the best.

Dara also means fear. The eyes of *Śreedevee* remove the fears. i.e., just by the sight of the long eyes of *Śreedevee* the fear is removed. Since **She** wants her compassionate benign look to fall on all the devotees, **she** has long eyes and **Her** retina waves here and there.

79th song of *Abhiraami Anthaadi* definitely states that *Sri Devi* gives everything to the devotees through her eyes only.

Verse #	50
Yantra with *Beeja* Letters	
Yantra Metal	Gold plate. The yantra can be drawn in sugar and consumed after japam.
Japa count #	1,000
# of Days	45
Daily offering	Sugar, Sugarcane
Result	To get rid off eye diseases.

*****

51. शिवे श‍ृङ्गारार्द्रा तदितरजने कुत्सनपरा
सरोषा गङ्गायां गिरिशचरिते विस्मयवती ।
हराहिभ्यो भीता सरसिरुह सौभाग्य जननी
सखीषु स्मेरा ते मयि जननि दृष्टिः सकरुणा ॥

Śivē Śruṅgārārdrā Taditarajanē Kutsanaparā
Sarōṣā Gaṅgāyāṃ Giriśacharitē Vismayavatī |
Harāhibhyō Bhītā Sarasiruha Saubhāgya Jananī
Sakhīṣu Smērā Tē Mayi Janani Dṛṣṭiḥ Sakaruṇā ||

This verse mentions, as *Śreedevee* gestures all the emotions one at a time excepting the tranquility emotion (which **She** always gestures).

Mother of all universe, the look from your eyes, is kind and filled with love, when looking at your Lord, is filled with hatred at all other men, is filled with anger when looking at Ganga, the other wife of your Lord, is filled with wonder, when hearing the stories of your Lord, is filled with fear, when seeing the snakes worn by your Lord, is filled with red colour of valour of the pretty lotus fine, is filled with jollity, when seeing your friends, and filled with mercy, when seeing me.

In *Lalita Sahasranama* 376th Name – **Shrungārarasasampoorṇā** – One who is filled with the essence of love. The word *Poorna* is referring to *Poorṇagiri Peeṭa*. It is said that *Poorṇagiri Peeṭa* resides in *Maṇipooraka* of the body. It may be remembered that it is the place of *Kāryabindu* and *Pashyanti* sound. It is important to note that in all special forms of *Śreedevee* the form of *Lalitāmbikā* form has the *Sringarā* (erotic) emotion as the main one.

The letter 'A' originated first and the other letters are all its varied forms. Again, the sweet taste originated first and the other five are formed from it. Similarly, *Sringāra* is the first emotion to origin and the other eight originated from it. That is, the other eight are the effects of *Sringāra* emotion. Hence it can be construed that, when **She** is full of the first emotion viz., *Sringāra,* **she** is full of the other eight also.

Srunga – main or chief, *Arara*   covering, that is to say the *Avidyā* (ignorance), which veils, *Sa* with *Sampoorṇa, Brahmam* (literal meaning perfect). The synopsis or the summary of the meaning of this name is that   **She** is both the conditioned and unconditioned *Brahmam*.

Again, in *Lalita Sahasranama* 799th Name – **Rasajnā** – One who knows all the ten tastes (expressions/ emotions). **She** is in the form of the tongue, which recognises the taste.

Oh! Mother of all universe, the look from your eyes, is kind and filled with love, when looking at your Lord, is filled with hatred at all other men, is filled with anger when looking at Ganga, the other wife of your Lord, is filled with wonder, when hearing the stories of your Lord, is filled with fear, when seeing the snakes worn by your Lord, is filled with red colour of valour of the pretty lotus fine, is filled with jollity, when seeing your friends and filled with mercy, when seeing me.

Verse #	51
Yantra with *Beeja* Letters	
Yantra Metal	Gold plate. The yantra can be drawn on Sandal paste and applied on the forehead after japam.
Japa count #	1,000
# of Days	45
Daily offering	Honey, black gram vadai
Result	To attract everyone

52. गते कर्णाभ्यर्णं गरुत इव पक्ष्माणि दधती
पुरां भेत्तु श्चित्तप्रशम रस विद्रावण फले ।
इमे नेत्रे गोत्राधरपति कुलोत्तं सकलिके
तवाकर्णाकृष्ट स्मरशर विलासं कलयतः॥

Gatē Karṇābhyarṇaṃ Garuta Iva Pakṣmāṇi Dadhatī
Purāṃ Bhēttu Śchittaprasama Rasa Vidrāvaṇa Phalē I
Imē Nētrē Gōtrādharapati Kulōttaṃ Sakalikē
Tavākarṇākṛṣṭa Smaraśara Vilāsaṃ Kalayataḥ II

Oh, flower bud, who is the head gear of the king of mountains, wearing black eye brows above, resembling the feathers of eagle and determined to destroy peace, from the mind of He who destroyed the three cities, your two eyes elongated up to thine ears, enact the arrows of the God of love.

In *Lalita Sahasranama* 601st Name – **Darāndolitadeerghākshee – One** who has wavering wide eyes extending upto her ears. *Dara* means a little/ slightly. The eyes of *Śreedevee* slightly waver on all sides. The eyes of *Śreedevee* are extended upto her ears. As per the characters declared in physiognomy the eyes extending upto the ears are the best.

Verse #	52
Yantra with *Beeja* Letters	रं
Yantra Metal	Gold plate.
Japa count #	1,000
# of Days	45
Daily offering	Till rice, payasam
Result	To get off all kinds of eyes and ears related diseases.

*****

53. विभक्त त्रैवर्ण्य व्यतिकरित लीलाञ्जनतया
विभाति त्वन्नेत्र त्रितय मिद मीशानदयिते ।
पुनः स्रष्टुं देवान् द्रुहिण हरि रुद्रानुपरतान्
रजः सत्वं बिभ्रत् तम इति गुणानां त्रयमिव ॥

Vibhakta Traivarṇyaṃ Vyatikarita Līlāñjanatayā
Vibhāti Tvannētra Tritaya Mida Mīśānadayitē ।
Punaḥ Sraṣṭuṃ Dēvān Druhiṇa Hari Rudrānuparatān
Rajaḥ Satvam Bhibhrat Tama Iti Guṇānāṃ Trayamiva ॥

Oh, Darling of Lord *Shiva*! Those three eyes of thine, coloured in three different shades (white, red and black), by the eye shades you wear, to enhance thine beauty, wear the three qualities of *sattva*, *rajas* and *tamas*, as if to recreate the holy trinity of *Vishnu*, *Brahma* and Rudra, after they merge and become one with you, during the final deluge.

Verse #	53
Yantra with *Beeja* Letters	ह्रीं
Yantra Metal	Gold plate – japam to be performed beneath a Deepa
Japa count #	1,000
# of Days	45
Daily offering	Milk payasam
Result	When the Deepa is so bright, Sri Devi will appear in front.

*****

54. पवित्रीकर्तुं नः पशुपति पराधीन हृदये
दयामित्रै नेत्रै ररुण धवल श्याम रुचिभिः ।
नदः शोणो गङ्गा तपनतनयेति ध्रुवममुम्
त्रयाणां तीर्थाना मुपनयसि सम्भेद मनघम् ॥

Pavitrīkartuṃ Naḥ Paśupati Parādhīna Hṛdayē
Dayāmitrai Rnētrai Raruṇa Dhavaḷa Śyāma Ruchibhiḥ I
Nadaḥ Śōṇō Gaṅgā Tapanatanayēti Dhruvamamum
Trayāṇāṃ Tīrthānā Mupanayasi Sambhēda Managham II

This verse is for destruction of all sins and curing of eye diseases.

She who has a heart owned by *Pashupathi*, your eyes which are the companions of mercy, coloured red, white and black, resemble the holy rivers, Saraswathi, which is red, Ganga which is white and Yamuna, the daughter of Sun, which is black and is the confluence of these holy rivers, which remove all sins of the world. We are certain and sure that you made this meet and join, to make us, who see you, as holy.

Verse #	54
Yantra with *Beeja* Letters	सां सां
Yantra Metal	Gold plate – the chakram can also be drawn in a cup of water and after japam the water can be drunk.
Japa count #	1,000
# of Days	45
Daily offering	Jaggery payasam
Result	For a healthy life

*****

55. निमेषोन्मेषाभ्यां प्रलयमुदयं याति जगति
तवेत्याहुः सन्तो धरणिधर राजन्यतनये ।
त्वदुन्मेषाज्जातं जगदिद मशेषं प्रलयतः
परेत्रातुं शंङ्गे परिहृत निमेषा स्तव दृशः ॥

Nimēṣōnmēṣābhyāṃ Pralayamudayaṃ Yāti Jagati
Tavētyāhuḥ Santō Dharaṇidhara Rājanyatanayē I
Tvadunmēṣājjātaṃ Jagadida Maśēṣam Pralayataḥ
Parētrātum Śaṃṅgē Parihṛta Nimēṣā Stava Dṛśaḥ II

Śree Ādi Śaṇkara, describes the same meaning with different interpretation as. How many fantasies about Sridevi's eyes? Differently in each verse – if *Śreedevee* closes **Her** eyes the entire world will be destroyed and hence **She** never closes **Her** eyes.

The learned sages tell, Oh! daughter of the king of mountain, that this world of us, is created and destroyed, when you open and shut, your soulful eyes. I believe my mother, that you never shut your eyes, so that this world created by you, never, ever faces deluge.

In *Lalita Sahasranama* 281st Name – **Unmesha Nimishotpanna Vipanna Bhuvanāvalee** – One who makes this world arise and disappear with the opening and shutting of **Her** eyes. Is it correct to say opening and closing of eyes relating to *Śreedevee,* since *Devas* do not blink their eyes? *Śreedevee* cannot be treated as belonging only to one race called *Devas*. Hence, the expression "opening and shutting" refer to the influence of the destiny of beings. This expression also means that **She** does the task of creation with so much ease, just by blinking **Her** eyes.

Verse #	55
Yantra with *Beeja* Letters	ब्लूं ब्लूं
Yantra Metal	Gold plate.
Japa count #	2,500
# of Days	45
Daily offering	Payasam, Coconut, betel leaves
Result	Enemies will become friendly

*****

56. तवापर्णे कर्णे जपनयन पैशुन्य चकिता
निलीयन्ते तोये नियत मनिमेषाः शफरिकाः ।
इयं च श्री बद्धच्छदपुटकवाटं कुवलयं
जहाति प्रत्यूषे निशि च विघटय्य प्रविशति ॥

Tavāparṇē Karṇē Japanayana Paiśunya Chakitā
Nilīyantē Tōyē Niyata Manimēṣāḥ Śapharikāḥ ।
Iyaṃ Cha Śrī Rbaddhachchada Puṭa Kavāṭaṃ Kuvalayaṃ
Jahāti Pratyūṣē Niśi Cha Vighaṭayya Praviśati ॥

Oh! She who is begotten to none, it is for sure that the black female fish in the stream are afraid to close their eyes. Fearing that thine long eyes, resembling them all, would murmur bad about them, in your ears to which they are close by. It is also for sure that the Goddess Lakshmi enters the blooming blue Lilly flowers (during day time), before your eyes close at night and reenter in the morning when they open.

Verse #	56
Yantra with *Beeja* Letters	
Yantra Metal	Gold plate.
Japa count #	20,000
# of Days	45
Daily offering	Any offering
Result	To remove the bondages

*****

57. दृशा द्राघीयस्या दरदलित नीलोत्पल रुचा
दवीयांसं दीनं स्नपय कृपया मामपि शिवे ।
अनेनायं धन्यो भवति न च ते हानिरियता
वने वा हर्म्ये वा समकर निपातो हिमकरः ॥

Dṛśā Drāghīyasyā Daradalita Nīlōtpala Ruchā
Davīyāṃsaṃ Dīnaṃ Snapaya Kṛpayā Māmapi Śivē ।
Anēnāyaṃ Dhanyō Bhavati Na Cha Tē Hāniriyatā
Vanē Vā Harmyē Vā Samakara Nipātō Himakaraḥ ॥

She who is the consort of Lord Shiva, please bathe me with your merciful look from your eyes which are very long and have the glitter of slightly opened, blue lotus flower divine. By this look, I will become rich with all that is known and you do not lose anything whatsoever, for does not the Moon shine alike, in the forest and in palaces great.

Verse #	57
Yantra with *Beeja* Letters	श्री श्री
Yantra Metal	Gold plate.
Japa count #	25,000
# of Days	45
Daily offering	Honey payasam
Result	All kinds of wealth

*****

58. अरालं ते पालीयुगल मगराजन्यतनये
न केषा माधत्ते कुसुमशर कोदण्ड कुतुकम् ।
तिरश्चीनो यत्र श्रवणपथ मुल्लङ्घ्य विलसन्
अपाङ्ग व्यासङ्गो दिशति शरसन्धान धिषणाम् ॥

Arālaṃ Tē Pālīyugala Magarājanyatanayē
Na Kēṣā Mādhattē Kusumaśara Kōdaṇḍa Kutukam |
Tiraśchīnō Yatra Śravaṇapatha Mullaṅghya Vilasan
Apāṅga Vyāsaṅgō Diśati Śarasandhāna Dhiṣaṇām ||

Oh goddess, daughter of king of mountains, who will not but believe that the two arched ridges between your eyes and ears are the flower bow of the God of Love? side glances of your eyes piercing through these spaces makes one wonder as if the arrows have been of Cupid sent through thine ears.

Kanchi Paramacharya's comment at this point is significant;

She will bless regardless of merit. The full Moon shines. Unappreciated by that difference everywhere pours the same nectarous Moon light – Moon pours Moonlit in the courtyard of Emperor's lofty palace. Similarly, Moon sheds light in the thorn bushes also. The comforts of the palace did not touch the Moon. As it fell in the forest, it was not pierced by a thorn. In this way, no matter where Ambal's blessings fall, there is no additional deficiency. If it falls on me, nothing will decrease. I will become full of its touch. You have no loss and I get immense gain. Adi Shankarar says, "Mother, swallow me up in your blessings".

When he said me 'too', he meant all of us included. Ambal, Ishvara and Acarya are one and the same. Acharya who has become like that has stood with us by his supreme mercy and has narrated this shloka for us. Ambal blesses her compassion, if you pray sincerely, even on those do not know anything; Her aura is as cold as the Moon and blue water lily. He shows us that it can uplift anyone.

Verse #	58
Yantra with *Beeja* Letters	
Yantra Metal	Gold plate. Ladies to wear nose stud with red stones.
Japa count #	5,000
# of Days	45
Daily offering	Honey, Mixed rice
Result	To attract everyone and for healthy life

*****

59. स्फुरद्गण्डाभोग प्रतिफलित ताटङ्क युगलं
चतुश्चक्रं मन्ये तव मुखमिदं मन्मथरथम् ।
यमारुह्य द्रुह्य त्यवनिरथ मर्केन्दुचरणं
महावीरो मार: प्रमथपतये सज्जितवते ॥

Sphuradgaṇḍābhōga Pratiphalita Tāṭaṅka Yugalaṃ
Chatuśchakram Manyē Tava Mukhamidam Manmatharatham |
Yamāruhya Druhya Tyavaniratha Markēnducharaṇaṃ
Mahāvīrō Māraḥ Pramathapatayē Sajjitavatē ||

I feel that thine face with the pair of ear studs, reflected in thine two mirrors like cheeks, is the four wheeled chariots of the God of love. Riding in this chariot of earth with Sun and Moon as wheels, perhaps he thought he can win Lord Shiva.

Verse #	59
Yantra with *Beeja* Letters	ऐं क्रीं सौः
Yantra Metal	Gold plate. After the japam the plate can be worn. Ladies can do japam by drawing the chakra in a turmeric paste and then apply on the face.
Japa count #	5,000
# of Days	45
Daily offering	Honey, Mixed rice
Result	To attract other sex.

*****

60. सरस्वत्याः सूक्ती रमृतलहरी कौशलहरीः
पिब्नत्याः शर्वाणि श्रवण चुलुकाभ्या मविरलम् ।
चमत्कार श्लाघाचलित शिरसः कुण्डलगणो
झणत्कारैस्तारैः प्रतिवचन माचष्ट इव ते ॥

Sarasvatyāḥ Sūktī Ramṛtalaharī Kauśalaharīḥ
Pibnatyāḥ Śarvāṇi Śravaṇa Chulukābhyā Maviralam I
Chamatkāra Ślāghāchalita Śirasaḥ Kuṇḍalagaṇo
Jhaṇatkāraistāraiḥ Prativachana Māchaṣṭa Iva Tē II

Oh Goddess! the consort of Lord Shiva, your sweet voice which resembles, the continuous waves of nectar, fills the ear vessels of Saraswathi, without break and she shakes her head hither and thither and the sound made by her ear studs appear as if they applaud your words.

Verse #	60
Yantra with *Beeja* Letters	श्री
Yantra Metal	Gold plate. After the japam the plate can be worn.
Japa count #	1,000
# of Days	45
Daily offering	Milk payasam
Result	To obtain speech and knowledge

*****

61. असौ नासावंश स्तुहिनगिरिवंश ध्वजपटि
त्वदीयो नेदीयः फलतु फल मस्माकमुचितम् ।
वहत्यन्तर्मुक्ताः शिशिरकर निश्वास गलितं
समृद्ध्या यत्तासां बहिरपि च मुक्तामणिधरः ॥

Asau Nāsāvaṃśa Stuhinagirivaṃśa Dhvajapaṭi
Tvadīyō Nēdīyaḥ Phalatu Phala Masmākamuchitam ǀ
Vahatyantarmuktāḥ Śiśirakara Niśvāsa Galitaṃ
Samṛddhyā Yattāsāṃ Bahirapi Cha Muktāmaṇidharaḥ ǁ

Oh Goddess! the flag of the clan of Himalayas, let your nose which is like a thin bamboo, give us the blessings which are apt and near. I feel mother, that you are wearing a rare pearl brought out by your breath, through your left nostril for your nose is a storehouse of rarest pearls divine.

Verse #	61
Yantra with *Beeja* Letters	
Yantra Metal	Gold plate. After the japam the plate can be worn.
Japa count #	12,000
# of Days	45
Daily offering	Mixed rice, coconut, fruits, Honey
Result	Success in all tasks.

*****

62. प्रकृत्या रक्ताया स्तव सुदति दन्तच्छदरुचेः
प्रवक्ष्ये सादृश्यं जनयतु फलं विद्रुमलता ।
न बिंबं तद्बिम्ब प्रतिफलन रागा दरुणितं
तुलामध्यारोढुं कथमिव विलज्जेत कलया ॥

Prakṛtyā Raktāyā Stava Sudati Dantachchadaruchēḥ
Pravakṣyē Sādṛśyaṃ Janayatu Phalaṃ Vidrumalatā I
Na Bimbaṃ Tadbimba Pratiphalana Rāgā Daruṇitaṃ
Tulāmadhyārōḍhuṃ Kathamiva Vilajjēta Kalayā II

Oh, goddess with beautiful rows of teeth, I tried to find a simile to your blood red lips and can only imagine the fruit of the coral vine! The fruits of the red cucurbit hang its head in shame, on being compared to your lips, as it has tried to imitate its colour from you and knows that it has failed miserably.

Verse #	62
Yantra with *Beeja* Letters	

Yantra Metal	Gold plate. After the japam the plate can be kept beneath the pillow while sleeping.
Japa count #	1,000
# of Days	45
Daily offering	Black gram rice
Result	Success in all tasks.

*****

63. स्मितज्योत्स्नाजालं तव वदनचन्द्रस्य पिबतां

चकोराणा मासी दतिरसतया चञ्चु जडिमा ।

अतस्ते शीतांशो रमृतलहरी माम्लरुचयः

पिबन्ती स्वच्छन्दं निशि निशि भृशं काञ्जि कधिया ॥

Smitajyōtsnājālaṃ Tava Vadanachandrasya Pibatāṃ
Chakōrāṇā Māsī Datirasatayā Chañchu Jaḍimā ।
Atastē Śītāṃśō Ramṛtalaharī Māmlaruchayaḥ
Pibantī Svachchandaṃ Niśi Niśi Bhṛśaṃ Kāñji Kadhiyā ॥

The Chakora[2] birds feel that their tongues have been numbed, by forever drinking the sweet nectar like light emanating from your Moon like face and for a change wanted to taste the sour rice gruel during the night and have started drinking the white rays of the full Moon in the sky.

Verse #	63
Yantra with *Beeja* Letters	ह्री
Yantra Metal	Gold plate. After the japam, the plate can be worn as a Talisman in the hip.
Japa count #	30,000
# of Days	30
Daily offering	Curd rice, honey, fruit, coconut
Result	Attracting of everybody.

*****

---

[2] A mythical bird which drinks Moon light

64. अविश्रान्तं पत्युर्गुणगण कथाम्रेडनजपा

जपापुष्पच्छाया तव जननि जिह्वा जयति सा ।

यदग्रासीनायाः स्फटिकदृष दच्छच्छविमयि

सरस्वत्या मूर्तिः परिणमति माणिक्यवपुषा ॥

Aviśrāntaṃ Patyurguṇagaṇa Kathāmrēḍanajapā
Japāpuṣpachchhāyā Tava Janani Jihvā Jayati Sā I
Yadagrāsīnāyāḥ Sphaṭikadṛsa Dachchhachchhavimayi
Sarasvatyā Mūrtiḥ Pariṇamati Māṇikyavapuṣā II

My Mother! The well known tongue of yours, which without rest chants and repeats the many goods of your Consort, Shiva, is red like the hibiscus flower. The Goddess of learning Saraswathi, sitting at the tip of your tongue, though white and sparkling like a crystal, turns red like the ruby, because of the colour of your tongue.

Verse #	64
Yantra with *Beeja* Letters	
Yantra Metal	Gold plate. After the japam, the plate can be worn, in a nose stud.
Japa count #	25,000
# of Days	18
Daily offering	Jaggery payasam
Result	Healthy life for ladies.

*****

65. रणे जित्वा दैत्या नपहृत शिरस्त्रैः कवचिभिः

निवृत्तै श्रण्डांश त्रिपुरहर निर्माल्य विमुखैः ।

विशाखेन्द्रोपेन्द्रैः शशिविशद कर्पूरशकला

विलीयन्ते मातस्तव वदनताम्बूल कबलाः ॥

Raṇē Jitvā Daityā Napahṛta Śirastraiḥ Kavachibhiḥ
Nivṛttai Śchaṇḍāṃśa Tripurahara Nirmālya Vimukhaiḥ ।
Viśākhēndrōpēndraiḥ Śaśiviśada Karpūraśakalā
Vilīyantē Mātastava Vadanatāmbūla Kabalāḥ ॥

Oh! mother of world, the lords Subramanya, Vishnu and Indra, returning and resting after the war with Asuras, have removed their head gear and wearing the iron jackets are not interested in the left over, after the worship of Shiva, which belongs to Chandikeswara. And are swallowing with zest, the half chewed betel, from your holy mouth, which has the camphor as white as the moon.

In *Lalita Sahasranama* 281st Name – **Tāmboolapooritamukhee** – One whose mouth is full of betel leaves. The specialty of *Śreedevee* chewing betel leaves was described in 26th name – *Karpooraveetikāmoda Samākarshi Digantara*.

Śree Ādi Śaṇkara, while interpreting the 14th name of *Sri Lalita Trishatee* – *Karpoora Veeti Sourabhya Kallolita Kakuptatā* – specially indicates as *Mahārāja Bogavatee*.

It is told that legendary poets, like *Kalidāsa*, *Kālamegha* and others, got their excellent capacity to write poems by consuming the juice of *Śreedevee's tāmboola* (betel leaves).

Verse #	65
Yantra with *Beeja* Letters	
Yantra Metal	Gold plate. After the japam, the plate can be worn.
Japa count #	1,000
# of Days	45
Daily offering	Any Offering
Result	Success in all tasks.

*****

66. विपञ्च्या गायन्ती विविध मपदानं पशुपते

स्त्वयारब्धे वक्तुं चलितशिरसा साधुवचने ।
तदीयै माधुर्यै रपलपित तन्त्रीकलरवां
निजां वीणां वाणी निचुलयति चोलेन निभृतम् ॥

Vipañchyā Gāyantī Vividha Mapadānaṃ Paśupatē
Stvayārabdhē Vaktuṃ Chalitaśirasā Sādhuvachanē I
Tadīyai Rmādhuryai Rapalapita Tantrīkalaravāṃ
Nijāṃ Vīṇāṃ Vāṇī Nichulayati Chōlēna Nibhṛtam II

Sarasvati sings the stories of *Parameshwara* in his Veena. You enjoy it and happily praise her. By hearing the sweetness of your voice, feeling shy, she puts her Veena in its cover.

Oh! mother of all, when you start nodding your head, muttering sweetly, "good, good", to the Goddess *Sarasvati*, when she sings the great stories to you, of Pashupathi our lord, with the accompaniment of her Veena, she mutes the Veena by the covering cloth, so that the strings throwing sweetest music, are not put to shame, by your voice full of sweetness.

In *Lalita Sahasranama* 27th Name – **Nijasallāpamādhurya Vinirbhartsita Kacchapee** – One whose sweet voice resembles the *Veena* (a string instrument) called *Kacchapi* in the hands of *Śree Sarasvati* (goddess of learning).

Kacchapi is the name of *Śree Sarasvati's* Veena. Normally, in any string instrument like *Veena*, only the musical notes will be heard and not the lyrics of a song. But since *Śree Sarasvati* is the embodiment of sound and music, the musical notes as well as the words in the lyrics are heard from her *Veena*. However, the words would not be explicit, but resemble the utterances of parrot and infants. *Śreedevee's* voice is so sweet, that it wins over the sweetness of *Śree Sarasvati's* Veena.

Again, in *Lalita Sahasranama* 857th Name – **Gānalolupā** – One who is fond of music. **She** is interested in vocal music, instrumental and *Sāma Gānam*.

Kālidāsa also says in his *Shyāmalādaṇḍaka* as; *Jaya Sangita Rasike*.

Verse #	66

Yantra with *Beeja* Letters	श्री श्री श्री
Yantra Metal	Gold plate.
Japa count #	5,000
# of Days	45
Daily offering	Rice
Result	Instrument and Vocal music knowledge

*****

67. कराग्रेण स्पृष्टं तुहिनगिरिणा वत्सलतया
गिरिशेनो दस्तं मुहुरधरपानाकुलतया ।
करग्राह्यां शम्भोर्मुखमुकुरवृन्तं गिरिसुते
कथंकारं ब्रूम स्तव चुबुकमोपम्यरहितम् ॥

Karāgrēṇa Spṛṣṭaṃ Tuhinagiriṇā Vatsalatayā
Giriśēnō Dastaṃ Muhuradharapānākulatayā |
Karagrāhyaṃ Śambhōrmukhamukuravṛntaṃ Girisutē
Kathaṅkāraṃ Brūma Stava Chubukamōpamyarahitam ‖

Oh! Daughter of the mountain, how can we describe the beauty of your chin, which was with affection caressed, by the tip of his fingers by your father Himavan; which was oft lifted by the Lord of the mountain, Shivā, in a hurry to drink deeply from your lips; which was so fit to be touched by his fingers; which did not have anything comparable, and which is the handle of the mirror of your face.

In *Lalita Sahasranama* 29th Name – ***Anākalita Sādrushya Chibukashree Virājitā*** – One who shines by virtue of the incomparable beauty of **Her** chin. Even the *Vāgdevees* (the goddess of words) could not find similes to describe the beauty of **Her** chin.

Verse #	67

Yantra with *Beeja* Letters	क्रीं श्रीं क्रीं क्रीं
Yantra Metal	Gold plate.
Japa count #	1,000
# of Days	45
Daily offering	Milk payasam, betel leaf
Result	King attraction

68. भुजाश्लेषान्नित्यं पुरदमयितुः कण्डकवती
तव ग्रीवा धत्ते मुखकमलनाल श्रियमियम् ।
स्वतः श्वेता काला गरु बहुल जम्बालमलिना
मृणालीलालित्यं वहति यदधो हारलतिका ॥

Bhujāślēṣānnityaṃ Puradamayituḥ Kaṇḍakavatī
Tava Grīvā Dhattē Mukhakamalanāla Śriyamiyam ।
Svataḥ Śvētā Kālā Garu Bahula Jambālamalinā
Mṛṇālīlālityaṃ Vahati Yadadhō Hāralatikā ॥

Oh! Mother, your neck appears full of thorns always, due to the hairs standing out, by the frequent embrace of thy Lord, who destroyed the three worlds. And looks like the beauty of the stalk of your lotus like face. The chain of white pearls worn below is dulled by the incense and myrrh and the paste of sandal applied there and is like the tender stalk dirtied by the bed of mud.

Verse #	68
Yantra with *Beeja* Letters	ह्रीं
Yantra Metal	Gold plate.
Japa count #	1,000
# of Days	45
Daily offering	Offering of choice

Result	To obtain Government benefits.

*****

69. गले रेखास्तिस्रो गति गमक गीतैक निपुणे
विवाह व्यानद्ध प्रगुणगुण सङ्ख्या प्रतिभुवः ।
विराजन्ते नानाविध मधुर रागाकर भुवां
त्रयाणां ग्रामाणां स्थिति नियम सीमान इव ते ॥

Galē Rēkhāstisrō Gati Gamaka Gītaika Nipuṇē
Vivāha Vyānaddha Praguṇaguṇa Saṅkhyā Pratibhuvaḥ ।
Virājantē Nānāvidha Madhura Rāgākara Bhuvāṃ
Trayāṇāṃ Grāmāṇāṃ Sthiti Niyama Sīmāna Iva Tē ॥

This verse describes these three lines in the neck of *Shree Devee*.

She who is an expert in *Gathi, Gamaka* and *Geetha*, the three lucky lines on your neck, perhaps remind one, of the number of the well tied manifold thread, tied during your marriage, and also remind of the place, in your pretty neck, where originates the three musical notes, of *Shadja, Madhyama* and *Gāndhara*.

In *Lalita Sahasranama* 924th Name – **Darasmeramukhāmbujā** – One whose lotus face is radiant with a sweet smile. It is the practice of poets to compare the face, feet, hands and eyes to Lotus flower. The below famous verse can be reminded;
Karāravindena Padāravindam Mukhāravinde Viniveshayantam ।
Vatasya Patrasya Pute Shayānam Bālam Mukuṇḍam Manasā Smarāmi ॥

The smile of *Śree Devee* has enhanced the beauty of the already beautiful face. **She** has attracted *Kāmeshwara* with this smile. **She** is already in the form of happiness. A drop of the happiness enjoyed by **Her** is seen as smile.

Dara – conch. Like the stem for Lotus flower, **her** conch like neck forms the stem of lotus like face. That neck shines well like conch. It is the practice of poets to compare the neck to a conch. The summary of this meaning – the head (the knowledge of *Brahmam*) is supported by the neck (*Praṇava*) is being advised by this name.

Dara in time of fear, *Smeramukha* **Her** face is always shinning, even in time of fear. The meaning is even at the time of final dissolution when all beings including the tri gods are being destroyed, **she** without any fear on **Her** face, continue to smile. **She** does not have fear. Even at that time, **she** witnesses the *tāndava* of *Maheshwara. Dare* – when it comes to protecting the devotees, **her** face is always gracious.

Verse #	69
Yantra with *Beeja* Letters	
Yantra Metal	Gold plate – couple should jointly perform japam.
Japa count #	1,000
# of Days	45
Daily offering	Coconut, fruits, betel leaf, honey
Result	Co operation among the couple. Success in all tasks.

*****

70. मृणाली मृद्वीनां तव भुजलतानां चतसृणां
चतुर्भिः सौन्दर्य सरसिजभवः स्तौति वदनैः ।
नखेभ्यः सन्त्रस्यन् प्रथम मथना दन्तकरिपोः
चतुर्णां शीर्षाणां सम मभयहस्तार्पण धिया ॥

Mrṇālī Mrdvīnāṃ Tava Bhujalatānāṃ Chatasrṇāṃ
Chaturbhiḥ Soundaryaṃ Sarasijabhavaḥ Stauti Vadanaiḥ |
Nakhēbhyaḥ Santrasyan Prathama Mathanā Dandhakaripōḥ
Chaturṇāṃ Śīrṣāṇāṃ Sama Mabhayahastārpaṇa Dhiyā ||

Brahma, the God born out of Lotus, afraid of the nails of Lord Shiva, who killed the Asura called Andhaka, which has clipped of one of his heads, praises with his four faces, your four pretty, tender hands, resembling the lotus flower stalk, so that he can ask for protection for his remaining four heads, by use of your four merciful hands at the same time.

Verse #	70
Yantra with *Beeja* Letters	

Yantra Metal	Gold plate – to be worn in hands.
Japa count #	1,000
# of Days	45
Daily offering	Yellow rice, betel leaf
Result	Success in all tasks.

*****

71. नखाना मुद्योतै र्नवनलिनरागं विहसतां
कराणां ते कान्तिं कथय कथयामः कथमुमे ।
कयाचिद्वा साम्यं भजतु कलया हन्त कमलं
यदि क्रीडल्लक्ष्मी चरणतल लाक्षारस चणम् ॥

Nakhānā Mudyōtai Rnavanalinarāgaṃ Vihasatāṃ
Karāṇāṃ Tē Kāntiṃ Kathaya Kathayāmaḥ Kathamumē I
Kayāchidvā Sāmyaṃ Bhajatu Kalayā Hanta Kamalaṃ
Yadi Krīḍallakṣmī Charaṇatala Lākṣārasa Chaṇam II

Oh, Goddess Uma, You only tell us how we can describe, the shining of your hands, by the light of your nails, which tease the redness of freshly opened lotus? Perhaps if the red lotus mixes, with the liquid mehandi adorning, the feet of Lakshmi, some resemblance can be seen.

Verse #	71
Yantra with *Beeja* Letters	
Yantra Metal	Gold plate – beneath a banyan tree.
Japa count #	12,000
# of Days	45
Daily offering	Offering of choice
Result	Yakhsinee attraction

*****

72. समं देवि स्कन्द द्विपवदन पीतं स्तनयुगं
तवेदं नः खेदं हरतु सततं प्रस्नुत मुखम् ।
यदालोक्याशङ्काकुलित हृदयो हासजनकः
स्वकुम्भौ हेरम्बः परिमृशति हस्तेन झटिति ॥

Samaṃ Dēvi Skanda Dvipavadana Pītaṃ Stanayugaṃ
Tavēdaṃ Naḥ Khēdaṃ Haratu Satataṃ Prasnuta Mukham ।
Yadālōkyāśaṅkākulita Hṛdayō Hāsajanakaḥ
Svakumbhau Hērambaḥ Parimṛśati Hastēna Jhaṭiti ॥

Our Goddess Devi, let your two cool breasts, which have faces that always, give out milk and are simultaneously drunk deeply, by Skanda and the elephant faced Ganesha, destroy all our sorrows. Seeing them and getting confused, the Herambha[3] feels for his two frontal globes to see whether they are there making you both laugh.

Verse #	72
Yantra with *Beeja* Letters	समं देवि ह्रीं ह्री
Yantra Metal	Gold plate – to be worn in a hand.
Japa count #	1,000
# of Days	45
Daily offering	Coconut, fruits, betel leaf, honey
Result	To get rid from all fears

*****

73. अमू ते वक्षोजौ अमृतरस माणिक्य कुतुपौ
न सन्देहस्पन्दो नगपति पताके मनसि नः ।
पिबन्तौ तौ यस्मा दविदित वधूसङ्ग रसिकौ
कुमारावद्यापि द्विरदवदन क्रौञ्च्दलनौ ॥

---

[3] Another name of Lord Ganesha

Amū Tē Vakṣōjou Amṛtarasa Māṇikya Kutupau
Na Sandēhaspandō Nagapati Patākē Manasi Naḥ ।
Pibantau Tau Yasmā Davidita Vadhūsaṅga Rasikau
Kumārāvadyāpi Dviradavadana Krauñchdalanau ॥

Oh, Victory flag of the king of mountains, we never have any doubt in our mind that your two breasts divine are the nectar filled pot made of rubies,
for the elephant faced one and he who killed Crownchasura[4], even today do not know the pleasure of women and remain as young children.

Verse #	73
Yantra with *Beeja* Letters	हां
Yantra Metal	Gold plate – or water – the same can be spread on ladies or cows and can be consumed by them.
Japa count #	1,000
# of Days	8
Daily offering	Honey
Result	To increase milk production

*****

74. वहत्यम्ब स्तंबेरम दनुज कुम्भप्रकृतिभिः
समारब्धां मुक्तामणिभिरमलां हारलतिकाम् ।
कुचाभोगो बिम्बाधर रुचिभि रन्तः शबलितां
प्रताप व्यामिश्रां पुरदमयितुः कीर्तिमिव ते ॥

Vahatyamba Stambērama Danuja Kumbhaprakṛtibhiḥ
Samārabdhāṃ Muktāmaṇibhiramalāṃ Hāralatikām ।
Kuchābhōgō Bimbādhara Ruchibhi Rantaḥ Śabalitāṃ
Pratāpa Vyāmiśrāṃ Puradamayituḥ Kīrtimiva Tē ॥

---

[4] Lord Subrahmanya killed the demon Crownchasura

Oh, my Mother! The center place of your holy breasts, wear the glittering chain, made out of the pearls, recovered from inside the head of Gajasura and reflect the redness of your lips, resembling the Bimba fruits and are coloured red inside. You wear the chain with fame, like you wear the fame of our Lord, who destroyed the three cities.

Verse #	74
Yantra with *Beeja* Letters	ऐं क्रीं सौः
Yantra Metal	Gold plate – or water – the same can be spread on ladies or cows and can be consumed by them.
Japa count #	108
# of Days	3
Daily offering	Milk payasam
Result	To get pride

*****

75. तव स्तन्यं मन्ये धरणिधरकन्ये हृदयतः
पयः पारावारः परिवहति सारस्वतमिव ।
दयावत्या दत्तं द्रविडशिशु आस्वाद्य तव यत्
कवीनां प्रौढाना मजनि कमनीयः कवयिता ॥

Tava Stanyaṃ Manyē Dharaṇidharakanyē Hṛdayataḥ
Payaḥ Pārāvāraḥ Parivahati Sārasvatamiva I
Dayāvatyā Dattaṃ Draviḍaśiśu Āsvādya Tava Yat
Kavīnāṃ Prauḍhānā Majani Kamanīyaḥ Kavayitā II

Oh, daughter of the king of mountains! I feel in my mind that the milk that flows from your breast, is really the goddess of learning, Saraswathi, in the form of a tidal wave of nectar. For, milk given by you, who is full of mercy, Made the child of Dravida (*Thirugnana Sambandar*), the king among those great poets, whose works stole one's mind.

From 71st onward, the last four verses described the beauty and glory of the breast of *Sri Devi*. In Sri Lalita Sahasranama also the same has been pronounced in more than one name. For instance, 33rd – ***Kāmeshvara Premaratna Maṇiprathi Paṇastanī*** – One who offers **Her** breasts as price (or in exchange) for the gem of love of *Śree Kāmeshwara*.

Verse #	75
Yantra with *Beeja* Letters	
Yantra Metal	Gold plate.
Japa count #	12,000
# of Days	45
Daily offering	Mixed rice, fruits
Result	To get pride

*****

76. हरक्रोध ज्वालावलिभि रवलीढेन वपुषा
गभीरे ते नाभीसरसि कृतसङ्गो मनसिजः ।
समुत्तस्थौ तस्मा दचलतनये धूमलतिका
जनस्तां जानीते तव जननि रोमावलिरिति ॥

Harakrōdha Jvālāvalibhi Ravalīḍhēna Vapuṣā
Gabhīrē Tē Nābhīsarasi Kṛtasaṅgō Manasijaḥ I
Samuttasthau Tasmā Dachalatanayē Dhūmalatikā
Janastāṃ Jānītē Tava Janani Rōmāvaliriti II

Oh, daughter of the mountain, the God of love who is the king of the mind, being lit by the flame of anger of Lord Shiva, immersed himself in the deep pond of thine navel. The tendril like smoke emanated from there and people think that this is the line of hair, that climbs from your navel upwards.

Verse #	76
Yantra with *Beeja* Letters	
Yantra Metal	Gold plate.
Japa count #	1,000
# of Days	10
Daily offering	Curd rice, coconut, fruits
Result	Success in all tasks

*****

77. यदेतत्कालिन्दी तनुतर तरङ्गाकृति शिवे
कृशे मध्ये किञ्चिज्जननि तव यद्भाति सुधियाम् ।
विमर्दा दन्योन्यं कुचकलशयो रन्तरगतं
तनूभूतं व्योम प्रविशदिव नाभिं कुहरिणीम् ॥

Yadētatkālindī Tanutara Taraṅgākṛti Śivē
Kṛśē Madhyē Kiñchijjanani Tava Yadbhāti Sudhiyām I
Vimardā Danyōnyaṃ Kuchakalaśayō Rantaragataṃ
Tanūbhūtaṃ Vyōma Praviśadiva Nābhiṃ Kuhariṇīm II

Oh! The mother of universe, who is Shiva and Shakthi, in the narrow part of the middle of your body, the learned men seem to see a line, which is in the shape of a small wave of the river Yamuna and which shines and glitters and appears like the sky made very thin by thine dense colliding breasts, entering your cave like navel.

Verse #	77
Yantra with *Beeja* Letters	

Yantra Metal	The chakram to be drawn and the shloka has to be written in the ashes of stem of lotus burnt. After the japam the ashes can be used as Vibhooti.
Japa count #	2,000
# of Days	15
Daily offering	Honey, fruits
Result	Attraction by all the people.

*****

78. स्थिरो गङ्गा वर्तः स्तनमुकुल रोमावलि लता
कलावालं कुण्डं कुसुमशर तेजो हुतभुजः ।
रते र्लीलागारं किमपि तव नाभिर्गिरिसुते
बेलद्वारं सिद्धे गिरिशनयनानां विजयते ॥

Sthirō Gaṅgā Vartaḥ Stanamukula Rōmāvali Latā
Kalāvālaṃ Kuṇḍaṃ Kusumaśara Tējō Hutabhujaḥ ।
Ratē Rlīlāgāraṃ Kimapi Tava Nābhirgirisutē
Biladvāraṃ Siddhē Rgiriśanayanānāṃ Vijayatē ॥

Oh! daughter of the mountain, is your navel a whirlpool in river Ganga, which looks very stable! Or is it the root of the climber, or the stream of your hair line, which has two breasts of yours as buds, or is it the *Homa* fire, where the fire is the light from Cupid, or is it the play house of Rathi, the wife of God of love, or is it the opening to the cave, in which Shiva's tapas gets fulfilled, I am not able to make up my mind.

Last three verses since 76th, describe the naval region of Sri Devi. In Sri Lalita Sahasranama also 34th Name – **Nābhyālavālaromālilatāphalakuchadvayee** – *Śreedevee*'s two breasts are like fruits in a creeper (line of hair) climbing from the trench (the naval). The deep naval is like a trench. The narrow line of hair grown upwards from the naval is like a creeper. The two breasts appear as if they are hanging from the creeper (an excellent metaphor).

Verse #	78
Yantra with *Beeja* Letters	
Yantra Metal	The chakram to be drawn and the shloka has to be written in the smelly sandal paste. After the japam the sandal can be used.
Japa count #	108
# of Days	45
Daily offering	Mixed rice, Black gram vadai
Result	Success in all tasks, Attraction towards King.

****

79. निसर्ग क्षीणस्य स्तनतट भरेण क्लमजुषो
नमन्मूर्ते नरीतिलक शनकै त्रुट्यत इव ।
चिरं ते मध्यस्य त्रुटित तटिनी तीर तरुणा
समावस्था स्थेम्नो भवतु कुशलं शैलतनये ॥

Nisarga Kṣīṇasya Stanataṭa Bharēṇa Klamajuṣō
Namanmūrtē Rnārītilaka Śanakai Truṭyata Iva ।
Chiraṃ Tē Madhyasya Truṭita Taṭinī Tīra Taruṇā
Samāvasthā Sthēmnō Bhavatu Kuśalaṃ Śailatanayē ॥

Oh! daughter of the mountain, you, the greatest among women, long live your pretty hips, which look fragile, which are by nature tiny, which are strained by your heavy breasts and hence slightly bent and which look like the tree in the eroded banks of a rushing river.

Verse #	79
Yantra with *Beeja* Letters	

Yantra Metal	Gold plate
Japa count #	1,000
# of Days	45
Daily offering	Milk payasam
Result	Success in all tasks.

*****

80. कुचौ सद्यः स्विद्य त्तटघटित कूर्पासभिदुरौ
कषन्तौ दोर्मूले कनककलशाभौ कलयता ।
तव त्रातुं भङ्गादलमिति वलग्नं तनुभुवा
त्रिधा नद्धं देवी त्रिवलि लवलीवल्लिभिरिव ॥

Kuchau Sadyaḥ Svidya Ttaṭaghaṭita Kūrpāsabhidurau
Kaṣantau Dormūlē Kanakakalaśābhau Kalayatā |
Tava Trātuṃ Bhaṅgādalamiti Valagnaṃ Tanubhuvā
Tridhā Naddahm Dēvī Trivali Lavalīvallibhiriva ||

Oh! Goddess, placed just below your shoulders, by Cupid, the God of love, tearing your blouse which is attached, to your body by the sweat, when you think of the greatness of your Lord, and resembling pots of Gold, your breasts appear to be tied by him, securely three times, by the three creeper like folds.

In *Sri Lalita Sahasranama* 36th name – ***Stana Bhāra Dalan Madhya Paṭṭa Bandha Valitrayā*** – One whose three folds in the abdominal area appear to be three bandages worn on the waist to prevent it from breaking due to the weight of the breasts. *Sāmudrika Shāstra* specifies that higher class men and women will have three lines (folds) on their forehead, neck and abdomen. They are signs of extremely good fortune.

Verse #	80
Yantra with *Beeja* Letters	
Yantra Metal	Gold plate – to be worn in the hand
Japa count #	1,000

# of Days	45
Daily offering	Any offering
Result	To obtain knowledge of subjects

*****

81. गुरुत्वं विस्तारं क्षितिधरपतिः पार्वति निजात्
नितम्बा दाच्छिद्य त्वयि हरण रूपेण निदधे ।
अतस्ते विस्तीर्णो गुरुरयमशेषां वसुमतीं
नितम्ब प्राग्भारः स्थगयति लघुत्वं नयति च ॥

Gurutvaṃ Vistāraṃ Kṣitidharapatiḥ Pārvati Nijāt
Nitambā Dāchchidya Tvayi Haraṇa Rūpēṇa Nidadhē ।
Atastē Vistīrṇō Gururayamaśēṣāṃ Vasumatīṃ
Nitamba Prāgbhāraḥ Sthagayati Laghutvaṃ Nayati Cha ॥

Oh, daughter of the mountain, perhaps Himavan, the king of mountains, gave readily as dowry to you, the density and breadth from his bottom, so that your behinds are broad and dense. And therefore, they both hide all the world and make the world light.

Verse #	81
Yantra with *Beeja* Letters	
Yantra Metal	Gold plate – to be facing South east
Japa count #	1,000
# of Days	16
Daily offering	Black gram vadai, jaggery payasam
Result	To extinguish fire

*****

82. करीन्द्राणां शुण्डान् कनककदली काण्डपटलीं
उभाभ्यामूरुभ्या मुभयमपि निर्जित्य भवति ।

सुवृत्ताभ्यां पत्युः प्रणतिकठिनाभ्यां गिरिसुते
विधिज्ञे जानुभ्यां विबुध करिकुम्भ द्वयमसि ॥

Karīndrāṇāṃ Śuṇḍān Kanakakadalī Kāṇḍapaṭalīṃ
Ubhābhyāmūrubhyā Mubhayamapi Nirjitya Bhavati ।
Suvṛttābhyāṃ Patyuḥ Praṇatikaṭhinābhyāṃ Girisutē
Vidhijjñē Jānubhyāṃ Vibudha Karikumbha Dvayamasi ॥

The reason for hardness of *Śreedevee*'s knees is stated this *verse*.

Oh! Daughter of the mountain, who knows the rules of the *Vedas*, using your two thighs, you have achieved victory over, the trunks of the elephant, and the Golden pseudo stem of group of Banana plants, and achieved victory over frontal globes, of Iravatha (the white elephant that arose from the ocean of milk when churned for nectar) the divine elephant, by your holy round knees, which have become hard, by repeated prostrations to your lord.

In *Sri Lalita Sahasranama* 39th name – *Kāmeshagyāta Soubhāgya Mārdavoru Dvayānvitā* – she has two beautiful and soft thighs known only to *Śree Kāmeshwara*. *Soubhāgyā* here means exquisiteness or beauty.

Again in *Sri Lalita Sahasranama* 40th name – **Māṇikya Mukuṭākāra Jānudvaya Virājitā – One** whose knees resemble hard, Red caps made of rubies. The knees are so Red and seem to be like a hard cap.

Verse #	82
Yantra with *Beeja* Letters	
Yantra Metal	Ashwi karna wooden plate – to be worn
Japa count #	1,000
# of Days	45
Daily offering	Grapes
Result	To extinguish flood

*****

83. पराजेतुं रुद्रं द्विगुणशरगर्भौ गिरिसुते
निषङ्गौ जङ्घे ते विषमविशिखो बाढ मकृत ।
यदग्रे दृश्यन्ते दशशरफलाः पादयुगली
नखाग्रच्छन्मानः सुर मकुट शाणैक निशिताः ॥

Parājētuṃ Rudraṃ Dviguṇaśaragarbhau Girisutē
Niṣaṅgau Jaṅghē Tē Viṣamaviśikhō Bāḍha Makṛta I
Yadagrē Dṛśyantē Daśaśaraphalāḥ Pādayugalī
Nakhāgrachchanmānaḥ Sura Makuṭa Śāṇaika Niśitāḥ II

Śree Ādi Śaṅkara says, that Cupid, who was burnt down by Lord *Shiva* was waiting for an opportunity to seek revenge on **Him**, and when **He** was attracted by *Śreedevee*'s beauty, Cupid made *Śreedevee*'s shanks his quiver and **Her** toes his arrows.

Oh! Daughter of the mountain, the five arrowed Cupid, to win, Rudra your lord, has made your legs, into an arrow case, with ten arrows. In the end of the case, are your two feet, studded with ten of your so called nails, which are the ten steel tipped arrows, sharpened on the crowns of *Devas*.

In *Sri Lalita Sahasranama* 41st name – **Indragopa Parikshipta Smaratooṇābha Janghikā** – One whose shank resembles Cupid's quiver surrounded by fireflies. A quiver is a case for carrying arrows, carried by the warriors, with a broad mouth and tapered at the bottom. The two shanks of *Sreedevee* are firm and reddish. This resembles Cupid's quiver surrounded by insects sparkling at night. The brightness of the ankles is enhanced by the sparkling insects. The reddish legs are glowing naturally, but as a metaphor this is compared to the fireflies shining in the night.

Verse #	83
Yantra with *Beeja* Letters	ॐ सुं ॐ
Yantra Metal	Gold plate – Archana with Hibiscus flower
Japa count #	1,000

# of Days	12
Daily offering	Honey jaggery payasam
Result	To avoid animal fear

*****

84. श्रुतीनां मूर्धानो दधति तव यौ शेखरतया
मातः शिरसि दयया देहि चरणौ ।
ययो: पाद्यं पाथः पशुपति जटाजूट तटिनी
ययो लार्क्षा लक्ष्मी ररुण हरिचूडामणि रुचि: ॥

Śrutīnāṃ Mūrdhānō Dadhati Tava Yau Śēkharatayā
Mamāpyētau Mātaḥ Śirasi Dayayā Dēhi Charaṇau I
Yayōḥ Pādyaṃ Pāthaḥ Paśupati Jaṭājūṭa Taṭinī
Yayō Rlākṣā Lakṣmī Raruṇa Harichūḍāmaṇi Ruchiḥ II

Oh, my mother, be pleased to place your two feet, which are the ornaments of the head of Upanishats, the water which washes them are the river Ganges, flowing from Shiva's head and the lac paint adorning, which have the red luster of the crown of Vishnu, on my head with compassion.

Verse #	84
Yantra with *Beeja* Letters	
Yantra Metal	Gold plate
Japa count #	1,000
# of Days	365
Daily offering	Honey, mixed rice, Milk payasam
Result	To move from one body to another

*****

85. नमो वाकं ब्रूमो नयन रमणीयाय पदयो:
तवास्मै द्वन्द्वाय स्फुट रुचि रसालक्तकवते ।

असूयत्यत्यन्तं यदभिहननाय स्पृहयते
पशूना मीशानः प्रमदवन कङ्केलितरवे ॥

Namō Vākaṃ Brūmō Nayana Ramaṇīyāya Padayōḥ
Tavāsmai Dvandvāya Sphuṭa Ruchi Rasālaktakavatē ।
Asūyatyatyantaṃ Yadabhihananāya Spṛhayatē
Paśūnā Mīśānaḥ Pramadavana Kaṅkēlitaravē ॥

We salute thine two sparkling feet, which are most beautiful to the eyes and painted by the juice of red cotton. We also know well that God of all living beings, your consort, is very jealous of the Asoka trees in the garden, which yearn for kick by your feet.

Verse #	85
Yantra with *Beeja* Letters	रं रं रं रं रं रं
Yantra Metal	Gold plate – Archana with red flowers
Japa count #	1,000
# of Days	12
Daily offering	Milk payasam
Result	To ward off all kinds of fear

*****

86. मृषा कृत्वा गोत्रस्खलन मथ वैलक्ष्यनमितं
ललाटे भर्तारं चरणकमले ताडयति ते ।
चिरादन्तः शल्यं दहनकृत मुन्मूलितवता
तुलाकोटिक्वाणैः किलिकिलित मीशान रिपुणा ॥

Mṛṣā Kṛtvā Gōtraskhalana Matha Vailakṣyanamitaṃ
Lalāṭē Bhartāraṃ Charaṇakamalē Tāḍayati Tē ।
Chirādantaḥ Śalyaṃ Dahanakṛta Munmūlitavatā
Tulākōṭikvāṇaiḥ Kilikilita Mīśāna Ripuṇā ॥

In a playful mood, after teasing you, about you and your family and at a loss to control your love tiff, when your consort does prostrations, your lotus like feet touches his forehead and the God of love, the enemy of your Lord, who was burnt by the fire from his third eye and was keeping the enmity with your lord like the ever hurting arrow, makes sounds like "Kili Kili", from your belled anklets on the legs.

Verse #	86
Yantra with *Beeja* Letters	यं यं यं
Yantra Metal	Gold plate – keep water in a pot and after japam take bath with that water
Japa count #	1,000
# of Days	21
Daily offering	Milk payasam, coconut, banana fruit
Result	To ward off all kinds of evil fear

*****

87. हिमानी हन्तव्यं हिमगिरिनिवासैक चतुरौ
निशायां निद्राणं निशि चरमभागे च विशदौ ।
वरं लक्ष्मीपात्रं श्रिय मतिसृजन्तौ समयिनां
सरोजं त्वत्पादौ जननि जयत श्चित्रमिह किम् ॥

Himānī Hantavyaṃ Himagirinivāsaika Chaturau
Niśāyāṃ Nidrāṇaṃ Niśi Charamabhāgē Cha Viśadau ।
Varaṃ Lakṣmīpātraṃ Śriya Matisṛjantou Samayināṃ
Sarōjaṃ Tvatpādau Janani Jayata Śchitramiha Kim ॥

Oh, my mother! The lotus flower rots in snow, but your feet are aces in being in snow. The lotus flower sleeps at night, but your feet are wakeful day and night. The lotus makes the goddess of wealth Lakshmi live in it, but your feet give Lakshmi (wealth) to the devotees and so your two feet always wins over the lotus. What is so surprising in this?

Verse #	87
Yantra with *Beeja* Letters	ह्रीं सर्प सर्प मं
Yantra Metal	The chakram has to be drawn and the shloka to be written in ashes from cremation ground –after japam the ashes can be used as Vibhooti.
Japa count #	1,000
# of Days	16
Daily offering	Milk payasam, coconut, fruits
Result	Attraction by everyone.

*****

88. पदं ते कीर्तीनां प्रपदमपदं देवि विपदां
कथं नीतं सद्भिः कठिन कमठी कर्पर तुलाम् ।
कथं वा बाहुभ्या मुपयमनकाले पुरभिदा
यदादाय न्यस्तं दृषदि दयमानेन मनसा ॥

Padaṃ Tē Kīrtīnāṃ Prapadamapadaṃ Dēvi Vipadāṃ
Kathaṃ Nītaṃ Sadbhiḥ Kaṭhina Kamaṭhī Karpara Tulām I
Kathaṃ Vā Bāhubhyā Mupayamanakālē Purabhidā
Yadādāya Nyastaṃ Dṛṣadi Dayamānēna Manasā II

This verse explicitly states that this simile is not the most appropriate one.

Oh, Goddess *Devee*, how did the poets compare, the foreside of your merciful feet, which are the source of fame to your devotees, and which are not the source of danger to them, to the hard shell of tortoise, I do not understand. How did he who destroyed the three cities, take them in his hand, and place them on hard rock, during your marriage?

In *Sri Lalita Sahasranama* 43rd name – ***Koorma Prushtha Jayishnu Prapadānvitā*** – One whose foot resembles a turtle's back. The back of the feet of higher class women would be pyramid like. In the absence of any other suitable comparison, turtle's back (though of an inferior class) is used as a simile.

Verse #	88
Yantra with *Beeja* Letters	
Yantra Metal	Gold plate
Japa count #	1,000
# of Days	180
Daily offering	Milk payasam, coconut, banana fruit
Result	To attract animals

*****

89. नखै नीकस्त्रीणां करकमल सङ्कोच शशिभिः
तरूणां दिव्यानां हसत इव ते चण्डि चरणौ ।
फलानि स्वःस्थेभ्यः किसलय कराग्रेण ददतां
दरिद्रेभ्यो भद्रां श्रियमनिश महाय ददतौ ॥

Nakhai Rnākastrīṇāṃ Karakamala Saṅkōcha Śaśibhiḥ
Taruṇāṃ Divyānāṃ Hasata Iva Tē Chaṇḍi Charaṇau ।
Phalāni Svaḥsthēbhyaḥ Kisalaya Karāgrēṇa Dadatāṃ
Daridrēbhyō Bhadrāṃ Śriyamaniśa Mahnāya Dadatau ॥

Your moon like nails, Oh mother who killed Chanda, which makes the celestial maidens, fold their hands in shame, forever tease your two feet, which unlike the holy trees in heaven, (which by their leaf bud like hands, give all they wish to the Gods) give the poor people wealth and happiness, always and fast.

Verse #	89
Yantra with *Beeja* Letters	
Yantra Metal	Gold plate – to wear the plate
Japa count #	1,000
# of Days	30

Daily offering	Jaggery payasam, Honey
Result	To get cured from any disease

*****

90. ददाने दीनेभ्यः श्रियमनिश माशानुसदृशीं
अमन्दं सौन्दर्यं प्रकर मकरन्दं विकिरति ।
तवास्मिन् मन्दार स्तबक सुभगे यातु चरणे
निमज्जन् मज्जीवः करणचरणः षट्चरणताम् ॥

Dadānē Dīnēbhyaḥ Śriyamaniśa Māśānusadṛśīṃ
Amandaṃ Soundaryaṃ Prakara Makarandaṃ Vikirati |
Tavāsmin Mandāra Stabaka Subhagē Yātu Charaṇē
Nimajjan Majjīvaḥ Karaṇacharaṇaḥ Ṣaṭcharaṇatām ||

My soul with six organs is similar to the six legged honey bees, which dip at your holy feet, which are as pretty as the flower bunch of the Celestial tree, which always grant wealth to the poor, whenever/ whatever they wish and which without break showers floral honey.

Note; From 84th, the past 7 verses describe the beauty and glory of the lotus feet of Sri Devi.

Verse #	90
Yantra with *Beeja* Letters	क्षां क्षां क्षीय क्षीय ह्री
Yantra Metal	Gold plate – the yantra and the verse can be written in Vibhooti and the same used after the japam
Japa count #	1,000
# of Days	30
Daily offering	Payasam, Honey
Result	To ward off all evils.

*****

91. पदन्यास क्रीडा परिचय मिवारब्धु मनसः
स्खलन्तस्ते खेलं भवनकलहंसा न जहति ।
अतस्तेषां शिक्षां सुभगमणि मञ्जीर रणित
च्छलादाचक्षाणं चरणकमलं चारुचरिते ॥

Padanyāsa Krīḍā Parichaya Mivārabdhu Manasaḥ
Skhalantastē Khēlaṃ Bhavanakalahaṃsā Na Jahati I
Atastēṣāṃ Śikṣāṃ Subhagamaṇi Mañjīra Raṇita
Chchalādāchakṣāṇaṃ Charaṇakamalaṃ Chārucharitē II

Śree Ādi Śaṇkara, describes that the swans are inspired by *Śreedevee*'s gait beauty and go behind **Her**. The swans in *Śreedevee*'s palace try to learn and copy the gait of *Śreedevee*. The soft sound of *Śreedevee*'s anklets seems to teach lessons to the swans.

She who has a holy life, the swans in your house, follows you without break, as if to learn, your gait, which is like a celestial play. Hence thine lotus like feet, taking recourse to the musical sound, produced by gems in your anklets, appears to teach them what they want.

In *Sri Lalita Sahasranama* 47th name – **Marāleemandagamanā** – One whose gait is slow and beautiful like a female swan. The gait of a swan is always soft and beautiful. The gait of a female swan is all the more graceful. Hence the female swan is compared. Everyone stands spellbound by the beauty of *Śreedevee* coming out of the sacrificial fire.

Again, in *Sri Lalita Sahasranama* 456th name – **Hamsinee** – One who is alongwith swans. Swan birds are famous for their beauty in walking. It is the practice of poets to compare the gait of great ladies to that of swan birds. (Great gentlemen's gait is compared to that of elephants or lions).

A type of *sannyasins* called *Paramahamsā* is indifferent to **Her** (i.e., those great *sannyasins* are always meditating upon **Her**), **She** is called as *Hamsinee*.

The exhale and inhale of breath together is called *Hamsa Mantra* or *Ajapā Mantra*. This is a *mantra* about *Śreedevee* and hence **She** is *Hamsinee*.

Verse #	91
Yantra with *Beeja* Letters	ॐ ह्रीं ह्रीं ह्रीं
Yantra Metal	Gold plate
Japa count #	2,000
# of Days	25
Daily offering	Any offering
Result	Immovable property or wealth

*****

92. गतास्ते मञ्चत्वं द्रुहिण हरि रुद्रेश्वर भृतः

शिवः स्वच्छ च्छाया घटित कपट प्रच्छदपटः ।

त्वदीयानां भासां प्रतिफलन रागारुणतया

शरीरी शृङ्गारो रस इव दृशां दोग्धि कुतुकम् ॥

Gatāstē Mañchatvaṃ Druhiṇa Hari Rudrēśvara Bhṛtaḥ
Śivaḥ Svachcha Chchāyā Ghaṭita Kapaṭa Prachchadapaṭaḥ I
Tvadīyānāṃ Bhāsāṃ Pratiphalana Rāgāruṇatayā
Śarīrī Śṛṅgārō Rasa Iva Dṛśāṃ Dōgdhi Kutukam II

Brahma, Vishnu, Rudra and Easwara, who are the gods who rule the world, become the four legs of your cot, so that they are able to serve you always. Sadāshiva who is white in colour, becomes the bedspread on which you sleep, and appears red, because he reflects your colour. And to your eyes which are the personification, of the feelings of love, he gives lot of happiness.

In *Sri Lalita Sahasranama* 309th name – **Ranjanee** – One who delights her devotees. **She** delights her devotees by providing bliss in this world and liberation in the other world. *Ranjayatee* means to make red. We all know that the colour of *Śreedevee* is red. For instance, the *dhyana* verse may be referred – by her presence, the rosy tinted *Devee* colours the pure *Paramashiva* as the red flower colours the crystal.

Again, in *Sri Lalita Sahasranama* 947th name – ***Panjca Pretamanjcādhi Shāyinee*** – One who is reclining on a couch made of five corpses. To indicate that **She** is greater than the five tasks (creation, protection, destruction, *tirodhāna* and *anugrahā*), the persons who do those tasks have been compared to the legs of the cot and its plank. *Brahma, Vishnu, Rudra* and *Eshvara* are the four legs of the couch and the *Sadāshiva* is the pure white sheet. **She** shines in that cot. These five are mentioned as corpses. They do their tasks through their respective *Shaktis* (energies) viz., *Vāmā, Jyeshtā*, etc. If the energies are not there, they cannot do anything. Hence, they are indicated as corpses.

It has been explained in the book called *Saparyāpattati Vāsanā* by *Śree Chidānanda Nātha* as;

#	Corpse	Energy	*Chakra*	God
1.	*Brahma Maya Manchapāda*	Creation	*Moolādhārā*	*Brahma*
2.	*Vişhņu Māyā Manchapāda*	Protection	*Swādishtānāna*	*Vişhņu.*
3.	*Rudra Maya Manchapāda*	Destruction	*Maņipoorakam*	*Rudra.*
4.	*Ěshwara Maya Manchapāda*	Complete Annihilation	*Anāhata*	*Ěshwara.*
5.	*Sadāshiva Manchapalakam*	*Anugraha*	*Vishuddhi*	*Sadāshiva.*

The corpse form of *Brahma, Vişhņu* and others has been explained in *Gnānārnavam* (verses 12 to 27);

Śree Devee said;
> *Pancha Pretān Maheshāna Bhroohi Teshām Tu Kāraņam |*
> *Nirjeevā Avināshāste Nityaroopāḥ Kadam Vibho ||*
> *Nirjeeve Nāsha Evāsti Te Katham Nityatām Gatāḥ |*

Eshwara said;
> *Sādhu Prushtam Tvayā BhadrePanchapretamayamKatham ||*
> *BrahmaVişhņushcha Rudrashcha Ěshwarashcha Sadāshivaḥ |*
> *Panchapretā Varārohe Nishchalā Eva Sarvadā ||*

Verse #	92
Yantra with *Beeja* Letters	
Yantra Metal	Gold plate
Japa count #	4,000
# of Days	30
Daily offering	Mixed rice
Result	To get back the kingdom

*****

93. अराला केशेषु प्रकृति सरला मन्दहसिते
शिरीषाभा चित्ते दृषदुपलशोभा कुचतटे ।
भृशं तन्वी मध्ये पृथु रुरसिजारोह विषये
जगत्रातुं शम्भो जयति करुणा काचिदरुणा ॥

Arālā Kēśēṣu Prakṛti Saralā Mandahasitē
Śirīṣābhā Chittē Dṛṣadupalaśōbhā Kuchataṭē ।
Bhṛṣaṃ Tanvī Madhyē Pṛthu Rurasijārōha Viṣayē
Jagattrātuṃ Śambhō Rjayati Karuṇā Kāchidaruṇā ॥

Her mercy which is beyond, the mind and words of our Lord Shiva, is forever victorious in the form of Aruna, so as to save this world. That spirit of mercy is in the form of Curves in her hairs, in the form of natural sweetness in her smile. In the form of pretty tenderness of a flower in her mind, in the form of firmness of a ruby stone in her breasts, in the form of thin seductiveness in her hips, in the form of voluptuousness in her breasts and back.

Verse #	93
Yantra with *Beeja* Letters	

Yantra Metal	Gold plate
Japa count #	2,000
# of Days	25
Daily offering	Honey
Result	To get all intentions satisfied

*****

94. कलङ्कः कस्तूरी रजनिकर बिम्बं जलमयं
कलाभिः कपूरै मरकतकरण्डं निबिडितम् ।
अतस्त्वद्भोगेन प्रतिदिनमिदं रिक्तकुहरं
विधि भूयो भूयो निबिडयति नूनं तव कृते ॥

Kalaṅkaḥ Kastūrī Rajanikara Bimbaṃ Jalamayaṃ
Kalābhiḥ Karpūrai Rmarakatakaraṇḍam Nibiḍitam I
Atastvadbhōgēna Pratidinamidaṃ Riktakuharaṃ
Vidhi Rbhūyō Bhūyō Nibiḍayati Nūnaṃ Tava Kṛtē II

The moon that we know is thine jewel box, filled with water of incense, the blackness we see in the Moon, the musk put for thy use in this box and the crescents we see of the Moon is thy canister of emerald, full of divine camphor. And for sure, Brahma the creator refills these daily, after your use, so that they are always full.

Verse #	94
Yantra with *Beeja* Letters	
Yantra Metal	Gold plate
Japa count #	1,000
# of Days	45
Daily offering	Mixed rice, fruits
Result	To get any legal wishes

*****

95. पुराराते रन्तः पुरमसि तत स्त्वच्चरणयोः
सपर्या मर्यादा तरलकरणाना मसुलभा ।
तथा ह्येते नीताः शतमखमुखाः सिद्धिमतुलां
तव द्वारोपान्तः स्थितिभि रणिमाद्याभि रमराः ॥

Purārātē Rantaḥ Puramasi Tata Stvaccaraṇayōḥ
Saparyā Maryādā Taralakaraṇānā Masulabhā I
Tathā Hyētē Nītāḥ Śatamakhamukhāḥ Siddhimatulāṃ
Tava Dvārōpāntaḥ Sthitibhi Raṇimādyābhi Ramarāḥ II

This verse says – to control the senses and to have focus in the mind lot of effort is required and it is very difficult.

You are the Leading light of the home of Lord Shiva, who destroyed the three cities, and so coming near you and worshipping at thine feet, are not for those with weak mind, who do not have control of their senses. And that is why perhaps, Indra and other Gods, stay outside your gates, and attain your sweet self, by practice of siddhis like *Anima*.

In *Sri Lalita Sahasranama* 771st name – **Durārādhyā** – One who is difficult to worship. **She** is difficult to worship for the incompetent and for those who cannot control their senses and sensory organs. Impossible to be worshipped by the fickle minded.

Verse #	95
Yantra with *Beeja* Letters	ॐ ह्रीं
Yantra Metal	Gold plate – to keep the plate in till oil. Japam should be made keeping the oil vessel on hand. After japam apply the oil on the wound.
Japa count #	108
# of Days	45
Daily offering	Till rice, Sugar
Result	To get any wound cured

96. कलत्रं वैधात्रं कतिकति भजन्ते न कवयः
श्रियो देव्याः को वा न भवति पतिः कैरपि धनैः ।
महादेवं हित्वा तव सति सतीना मचरमे
कुचाभ्या मासङ्गः कुरवक तरो रप्यसुलभः ॥

Kalatraṃ Vaidhātraṃ Katikati Bhajantē Na Kavayaḥ
Śriyō Dēvyāḥ Kō Vā Na Bhavati Patiḥ Kairapi Dhanaiḥ |
Mahādēvaṃ Hitvā Tava Sati Satīnā Macharamē
Kuchābhyā Māsaṅgaḥ Kuravaka Tarō Rapyasulabhaḥ ||

Śree Ādi Śaṇkara, describes that since *Śreedevee* has never had a consort other than Lord *Parameshwara,* **her** *pativrata* is much special than anybody else's.

Many poets reach the Goddess of learning, the wife of the creator, by composing soulful poems. Many devotees, who search and attain riches, are termed as the Lord of the Goddess of wealth. Oh, first among chaste woman, except Lord Shiva your consort, your breasts have not even touched, the holy henna tree.

In *Sri Lalita Sahasranama* 128th name – **Sādhvee** – One who is paragon of virtue. The pride of loyalty to her consort by *Śreedevee* is specially mentioned in this name. When *Daksha,* father of *Śreedevee* (in one of **Her** incarnations) despised **Her** consort, Lord *Shiva,* **she** could not tolerate it and left **Her** body. **She** took another incarnation as daughter of *Himavān,* did penance and got Lord *Parameswara's* hand. This is a famous story known to all. There are other places too where *Śreedevee* did penance and married Lord *Parameshwara* (for instance Mylapore and Mangadu in Chennai, India). It is specifically mentioned that *Śreedevee* did not marry anybody else anytime (in any of the incarnations also).

Again, in *Sri Lalita Sahasranama* 820th name – **Satee** – One who is a great *pativrata.* Or **She** is in the form of *Sat. Satee* is a causal name for *Dākshāyanee,* daughter of *Dakshan. Brahma Purāṇa* says about the daughter of *Himavān,* "**She** was earlier as *Satee Devee,* becomes *Uma,* always with *Shiva* and never moves out of him";

Sātu Devee Satee Poorvamāseet Pashchādumābhavat |
Sahavratā Bhavasyaiva Naitayā Muchayate Bhavaḥ ||

Verse #	96
Yantra with *Beeja* Letters	
Yantra Metal	Gold plate
Japa count #	1,000
# of Days	45
Daily offering	Milk payasam
Result	To become a drawing artist

*****

97. गिरामाहु देवीं द्रुहिणगृहिणी मागमविदो
हरे: पत्नीं पद्मां हरसहचरी मद्रितनयाम् ।
तुरीया कापि त्वं दुरधिगम निस्सीम महिमा
महामाया विश्वं भ्रमयसि परब्रह्ममहिषि ॥

Girāmāhu Rdēvīṃ Druhiṇagṛhiṇī Māgamavidō
Harēḥ Patnīṃ Padmāṃ Harasahacharī Madritanayām I
Turīyā Kāpi Tvaṃ Duradhigama Nissīma Mahimā
Mahāmāyā Viśvaṃ Bhramayasi Parabrahmamahiṣi II

It is mentioned as the *Sadāshiva* form is above *Brahma, Viṣhṇu* and *Rudra* – the fourth form *Mahāmāyā* is above the three forms *Sarasvati, Lakshmi* and *Parvathi.*

Oh, *Parāshakti*, who is one with *Parabrahmam*, though those who have learned *Vedas*, call you as Brahma's consort Saraswathi, or call you as Vishnu's consort Lakshmi, or call you as Shiva's consort Parvathi, you are the fourth called *Mahā Māyā*, who gives life to the world, and have attained all that is to attain.

In *Sri Lalita Sahasranama* 843rd name – **Bhavacakrapravartinee** – One who controls the wheel of trans migratory existence (*samsara*). *Manu Smriti* (XII 124) says – he rotates, like a wheel, all the living beings, in the form of the five primary elements earth, water, fire, air and ether, through birth, growth and waning;
Esha Sarvāni Bhootāni Panchabhirvyāpya Moortibhiḥ I
Janma Vruddhi Kshayair Nityam Samsārāyati Chakravat II

In *Viṣhṇu Bhagavatam* also we read as – you are the head of all the bondages in the world and also the remover of those bondages. The wise and those who surrender to you, worship you to get rid of the pains;

Tvameva Sarvajagatām Eshvaro Bandhamokshayoḥ ।
Tam Tvām Archaṇti Kushalāḥ Prapannārtiharam Haram ॥

Verse #	97
Yantra with *Beeja* Letters	
Yantra Metal	Gold plate
Japa count #	1,000
# of Days	45
Daily offering	Rice, honey
Result	To become speech expert

*****

98. कदा काले मातः कथय कलितालक्तकरसं
पिबेयं विद्यार्थी तव चरण निर्णेजनजलम् ।
प्रकृत्या मूकानामपि च कविता०कारणतया
कदा धत्ते वाणीमुखकमल ताम्बूल रसताम् ॥

Kadā Kālē Mātaḥ Kathaya Kalitālaktakarasaṃ
Pibēyaṃ Vidyārthī Tava Charaṇa Nirṇējanajalam ।
Prakṛtyā Mūkānāmapi Cha Kavitā0kāraṇatayā
Kadā Dhattē Vāṇīmukhakamala Tāmbūla Rasatām ॥

Oh, my mother! When shall I, who beg for knowledge be able to drink, the nectar like water, flowing from your feet, mixed with reddish mehandi applied there? When shall that water attain the goodness of saliva mixed with Thambola (betel leaves) from the mouth of goddess of learning, which made one born as mute into the king of poets?

Verse #	98
Yantra with *Beeja* Letters	ह्रीं
Yantra Metal	Gold plate
Japa count #	1,000
# of Days	45
Daily offering	Any offering
Result	Ladies to become pregnant, gents to get anything of choice

*****

99. सरस्वत्या लक्ष्म्या विधि हरि सपत्नो विहरते
रतेः पातिव्रत्यं शिथिलयति रम्येण वपुषा ।
चिरं जीवन्नेव क्षपित पशुपाश व्यतिकरः
परानन्दाभिख्यं रसयति रसं त्वद्भजनवान् ॥

Sarasvatyā Lakṣmyā Vidhi Hari Sapatnō Viharatē
Ratēḥ Pātivratyaṃ Śithilayati Ramyēṇa Vapuṣā I
Chiraṃ Jīvannēva Kṣapita Paśupāśa Vyatikaraḥ
Parānandābhikhyaṃ Rasayati Rasaṃ Tvadbhajanavān II

Those who worship thee, Oh! mother, are so learned and so rich, that even Brahma and Vishnu, are jealous of them they are so handsome, that even the wife of Cupid, Rathi, yearns for them. He unbound from the ties of this birth, always enjoys ecstatic happiness, and lives forever.

In *Sri Lalita Sahasranama* 614th name – **Sachāmara Ramāvāṇee Savyadakshiṇa Sevitā** – One who is attended on either side by *Lakshmi* and *Sarasvati* holding *chāmaras* (hand fans). It has been mentioned that *Lakshmi* and *Sarasvati* serve *Śreedevee* on both the sides. A devotee of *Śreedevee* also becomes merged with *Śreedevee*. Hence this indicates that *Lakshmi* and *Sarasvati* bless/ serve the devotees of *Śreedevee* also. In general, *Savya* means right side. Since right side has been mentioned by the word *Dakshiṇa*, the word *Savya* has been taken as left side.

Verse #	99
Yantra with *Beeja* Letters	ह्रीं
Yantra Metal	Gold plate – to wear the plate
Japa count #	1,000
# of Days	15
Daily offering	Mixed rice, black gram vadai
Result	To get a comfortable life

*****

100. प्रदीप ज्वालाभि दिवसकर नीराजनविधिः
सुधासूते श्रन्द्रोपल जललवै रघ्यरचना ।
स्वकीयैरम्भोभिः सलिल निधि सौहित्यकरणं
त्वदीयाभि र्वाग्भि स्तव जननि वाचां स्तुतिरियम् ॥

Pradīpa Jvālābhi Rdivasakara Nīrājanavidhiḥ
Sudhāsūtē Śchandrōpala Jalalavai Raghyarachanā |
Svakīyairambhōbhiḥ Salila Nidhi Sauhityakaraṇaṃ
Tvadīyābhi Rvāgbhi Stava Janani Vāchāṃ Stutiriyam ||

Śree Ādi Śaṅkara says, that all types of letters, words and speeches belong to *Śreedevee* only.

Oh! Goddess who is the source of all words, this poem which is made of words, that you only made, is like showing the camphor lamp to the Sun, is like offering as ablation to the Moon, the water got from the Moon stone, and is like offering water worship, to the sea.

In *Sri Lalita Sahasranama* 640th name – **Vāgadheeshvaree** – One who is the head of speech. **She** is the head of the eight *Vasinee* and other *Vāg Devees*. That is the reason, they wrote this *Sahasranāma*, by **Her** order. **She** has *Vāgvādinee*, who is the head of speech and letters, as her part. Hence *Vāgadheeshvaree*.

Verse #	100
Yantra with *Beeja* Letters	
Yantra Metal	Gold plate
Japa count #	1,000
# of Days	16
Daily offering	Three types of sweets, Jamun fruit
Result	To successfully complete all tasks

Thus, we have got 100 verses as 100 magical treasures of mantras. These appear to be a eulogy to *Sri Devi* when read superficially. But there are many theological ideas and philosophies embedded in them. The first 41 of these verses deal with the *Sri Chakra* and the 6 *Chakras* and 3 *Granthis* in our body – above all the *Sahasrara Chakra*.

The remaining 59 verses – 42 to 100 verses – starting with the controversy over whether the hair is naturally fragrant – the forehead, eyebrows, eyes, cheeks, ears, lips, speech, neck, breasts, abdomen, hips, thighs, knees, ankles – The soles of the feet, the toes and the dust of the feet below were atomically, described bit by bit. *Sri Adi Shankara* has brought *Sri Devi*, as he saw, as it is before our eyes. He has shared that privilege with us with the aim of increasing the pleasure he has seen. What a comment! What metaphors! What an experience! What bliss! We are all very much blessed. We do not want to come out of swimming in the ocean of nectar.

Phala Shruti – Results

सौन्दर्ययलहरि मुख्यस्तोत्रं संवार्तदायकम् ।
भगवद्पाद सन्क्लुप्तं पठेन् मुक्तौ भवेन्नरः ॥

Soundaryalahari Mukhyastōtram Saṃvārtadāyakam ।
Bhagavadpāda Sankluptaṃ Paṭhēn Muktau Bhavēnnaraḥ ॥

May Sri Devi shower all kinds of benefits to those who read and listen whole heartedly, with attention and focus to this Soundaryalahari Slogam authored by Srimad Adi Shankara Bhagavat Badal.

॥ सौन्दर्यलहरि स्तोत्रं सम्पूर्ण ॥ *Iti Soundaryalahari Stōtraṃ Sampūrṇaṃ* ॥

*****

Soundaryalahari – Verses – Samskrutam

भुमौस्खलित पादानाम् भूमिरेवा वलम्बनम् ।
त्वयी जाता पराधानाम् त्वमेव शरणम् शिवे ॥

शिवः शक्त्या युक्तो यदि भवति शक्तः प्रभवितुं
न चेदेवं देवो न खलु कुशलः स्पन्दितुमपि ।
अतस्त्वाम् आराध्यां हरि हर विरिञ्चादि भिरपि
प्रणन्तुं स्तोतुं वा कथ मकृत पुण्यः प्रभवति ॥ 1

तनीयांसुं पांसुं तव चरण पङ्केरुह भवं
विरिञ्चिः सञ्चिन्वन् विरचयति लोका नविकलम् ।
वहत्येनं शौरिः कथमपि सहस्रेण शिरसां
हरः सङ्क्षुद् यैनं भजति भसितोद्धूल नविधिम् ॥ 2

अविद्याना मन्त स्तिमिर मिहिर द्वीपनगरी
जडानां चैतन्य स्तबक मकरन्द श्रुतिझरी ।
दरिद्राणां चिन्तामणि गुणनिका जन्मजलधौ
निमग्नानां दंष्ट्रा मुररिपु वराहस्य भवति ॥ 3

त्वदन्यः पाणिभ्यामभयवरदो दैवतगणः
त्वमेका नैवासि प्रकटित वराभीत्यभिनया ।
भयात् त्रातुं दातुं फलमपि च वांछासमधिकं
शरण्ये लोकानां तव हि चरणावेव निपुणौ ॥ 4

हरिस्त्वामारध्य प्रणत जन सौभाग्य जननीं
पुरा नारी भूत्वा पुररिपुमपि क्षोभ मनयत् ।
स्मरोऽपि त्वां नत्वा रतिनयन लेह्येन वपुषा
मुनीनामप्यन्तः प्रभवति हि मोहाय महताम् ॥ 5

धनुः पौष्पं मौर्वी मधुकरमयी पञ्च विशिखाः
वसन्तः सामन्तो मलयमरुदायोधन रथः ।
तथाप्येकः सर्वं हिमगिरिसुते कामपि कृपां
अपाङ्गात्ते लब्ध्वा जगदिद मनङ्गो विजयते ॥ 6

क्वणत्काञ्ची दामा करि कलभ कुम्भ स्तननता
परिक्षीणा मध्ये परिणत शरच्चन्द्र वदना ।
धनुर्बाणान् पाशं सृणिमपि दधाना करतलैः
पुरस्ता दास्तां नः पुरमथितु राहो पुरुषिका ॥ 7

सुधासिन्धोर्मध्ये सुरविट पिवाटी परिवृते
मणिद्वीपे नीपो पवनवति चिन्तामणि गृहे ।
शिवाकारे मञ्चे परमशिव पर्यङ्क निलयाम्
भजन्ति त्वां धन्याः कतिचन चिदानन्द लहरीम् ॥ 8

महीं मूलाधारे कमपि मणिपूरे हुतवहं
स्थितं स्वधिष्टाने हृदि मरुत माकाश मुपरि ।
मनोऽपि भ्रूमध्ये सकलमपि भित्वा कुलपथं
सहस्रारे पद्मे स हरहसि पत्या विहरसे ॥ 9

सुधाधारासारै श्ररणयुगलान्त र्विगलितैः
प्रपञ्चं सिञ्न्ती पुनरपि रसाम्नाय महसः ।
अवाप्य स्वां भूमिं भुजगनिभ मध्युष्ट वलयं
स्वमात्मानं कृत्वा स्वपिषि कुलकुण्डे कुहरिणि ॥ 10

चतुर्भिः श्रीकण्ठैः शिवयुवतिभिः पञ्चभिरपि
प्रभिन्नाभिः शम्भोर्नवभिरपि मूलप्रकृतिभिः ।
चतुश्चत्वारिंशद् वसुदल कलाश्च त्रिवलय
त्रिरेखाभिः सार्धं तव शरणकोणाः परिणताः ॥ 11

त्वदीयं सौन्दर्यं तुहिनगिरिकन्ये तुलयितुं
कवीन्द्राः कल्पन्ते कथमपि विरिञ्चि प्रभृतयः ।
यदालोकौत्सुक्या दमरललना यान्ति मनसा
तपोभिर्दुष्प्रापामपि गिरिश सायुज्य पदवीम् ॥ 12

नरं वर्षीयांसं नयनविरसं नर्मसु जडं
तवापाङ्गालोके पतित मनुधावन्ति शतशः ।
गलद्वेणीबन्धाः कुचकलश विस्त्रिस्त सिचया
हठात् त्रुट्यत्काञ्यो विगलित दुकूला युवतयः ॥ 13

क्षितौ षट्पञ्चाशद् द्विसमधिक पञ्चाश दुदके
हुताशे द्वाषष्टि श्चतुरधिक पञ्चाश दनिले ।
दिवि द्विः षट् त्रिंशत् मनसि च चतुःषष्टिरिति ये
मयूखा स्तेषा मप्युपरि तव पादाम्बुज युगम् ॥ 14

शरज्ज्योत्स्ना शुद्धां शशियुत जटाजूट मकुटां
वर त्रास त्राण स्फटिकघटिका पुस्तक कराम् ।
सकृन्न त्वा नत्वा कथमिव सतां सन्निदधते
मधु क्षीर द्राक्षा मधुरिम धुरीणाः फणितयः ॥ 15

कवीन्द्राणां चेतः कमलवन बालातप रुचिं
भजन्ते ये सन्तः कतिचिदरुणामेव भवतीम् ।
विरिञ्चि प्रेयस्या स्तरुणतर श्रृङ्गार लहरी
गभीराभि र्वाग्भिः विदधति सतां रञ्जनममी ॥ 16

सवित्रीभि र्वाचां चशि मणि शिला भङ्ग रुचिभि
र्वशिन्यद्याभि स्त्वां सह जननि सञ्चिन्तयति यः ।
स कर्ता काव्यानां भवति महतां भङ्गिरुचिभि
र्वचोभि र्वाग्देवी वदन कमलामोद मधुरैः ॥ 17

तनुच्छायाभिस्ते तरुण तरणि श्रीसरणिभिः
दिवं सर्वां उर्वीं अरुणिमनि मग्नां स्मरति यः ।
भवन्त्यस्य त्रस्य द्वनहरिण शालीन नयनाः
सहोर्वश्या वश्याः कति कति न गीर्वाण गणिकाः ॥ 18

मुखं बिन्दुं कृत्वा कुचयुगमध स्तस्य तदधः
हरार्धं ध्यायेद्यः हरमहिषि ते मन्मथकलाम् ।
स सद्यः सङ्क्षोभं नयति वनिता इत्यतिलघु
त्रिलोकीमप्याशु भ्रमयति रवीन्दु स्तनयुगाम् ॥ 19

किरन्ती मङ्गेभ्यः किरण निकुरुम्बामृतरसं
हृदि त्वा माधत्ते हिमकरशिला मूर्तिमिव यः ।
स सर्पाणां दर्पं शमयति शकुन्ताधिप इव
ज्वरप्लुष्टान् दृष्ट्या सुखयति सुधाधारसिरया ॥ 20

तटिल्लेखा तन्वीं तपन शशि वैश्वानर मयीं
निषण्णां षण्णामप्युपरि कमलानां तव कलाम् ।
महापद्माटव्यां मृदित मलमायेन मनसा
महान्तः पश्यन्तो दधति परमाह्लाद लहरीम् ॥ 21

भवानि त्वं दासे मयि वितर दृष्टिं सकरुणां
इति स्तोतुं वाञ्छन् कथयति भवानि त्वमिति यः ।
तदैव त्वं तस्मै दिशसि निजसायुज्य पदवीं
मुकुन्द ब्रह्मेन्द्र स्फुट मकुट नीराजितपदाम् ॥ 22

त्वया हत्वा वामं वपु रपरितृप्तेन मनसा
शरीरार्धं शम्भोः अपरमपि शङ्के हृतमभूत् ।
यदेतत् त्वद्रूपं सकलमरुणाभं त्रिनयनं
कुचाभ्यामानम्रं कुटिल शशिचूडाल मकुटम् ॥ 23

जगत्सूते धाता हरिखति रुद्रः क्षपयते
तिरस्कुर्व न्नेतत् स्वमपि वपु रीश स्तिरयति ।
सदा पूर्वः सर्व तदिद मनुगृह्णाति च शिव
स्तवाज्ञां आलम्ब्य क्षणचलितयो भ्रूलतिकयोः ॥ 24

त्रयाणां देवानां त्रिगुण जनितानां तव शिवे
भवेत् पूजा पूजा तव चरणयो र्या विरचिता ।
तथा हि त्वत्पादोद्वहन मणिपीठस्य निकटे
स्थिता ह्येते शश्वन्मुकुलित करोत्तंस मकुटाः ॥ 25

विरिञ्चिः पञ्चत्वं व्रजति हरिराप्नोति विरतिं
विनाशं कीनाशो भजति धनदो याति निधनम् ।
वितन्द्री माहेन्द्री विततिरपि संमीलित दृशा
महासंहारेऽस्मिन् विहरति सति त्वत्पति रसौ ॥ 26

जपो जल्पः शिल्पं सकलमपि मुद्राविरचना
गतिः प्रादक्षिण्य क्रमण मशनाद्याहुति विधिः ।
प्रणामः संवेशः सुखमखिल मात्मार्पण दृशा
सपर्या पर्याय स्तव भवतु यन्मे विलसितम् ॥ 27

सुधामप्यास्वाद्य प्रति भय जरामृत्यु हरिणीं
विपद्यन्ते विश्वे विधि शतमखाद्या दिविषदः ।
करालं यत्क्ष्वेलं कबलितवतः कालकलना
न शम्भोस्तन्मूलं तव जननि ताटङ्क महिमा ॥ 28

किरीटं वैरिञ्चं परिहर पुरः कैटभभिदः
कठोरे कोटीरे स्कलसि जहि जम्भारि मकुटम् ।
प्रणम्रेष्वेतेषु प्रसभ मुपयातस्य भवनं
भवस्याभ्युत्थाने तव परिजनोक्ति र्विजयते ॥ 29

स्वदेहोद्भूताभि र्घृणिभि रणिमाद्याभि रभितो
निषेव्ये नित्ये त्वा महमिति सदा भावयति यः ।
किमाश्चर्यं तस्य त्रिनयन समृद्धिं तृणयतो
महासंवर्तार्ग्नि र्विरचयति नीराजनविधिम् ॥ ३०

चतुः षष्ट्या तन्त्रैः सकल मतिसन्धाय भुवनं
स्थितस्तत्त सिद्धि प्रसव परतन्त्रैः पशुपतिः ।
पुनस्त्व न्निर्बन्धा दखिल पुरुषार्थैक घटना
स्वतन्त्रं ते तन्त्रं क्षितितल मवातीतरदिदम् ॥ ३१

शिवः शक्तिः कामः क्षिति रथ रविः शीतकिरणः
स्मरो हंसः शक्र स्तदनु च परा मार हरयः ।
अमी हृल्लेखाभि स्तिसृभि रवसानेषु घटिताः
भजन्ते वर्णास्ते तव जननि नामावयवताम् ॥ ३२

स्मरं योनिं लक्ष्मीं त्रितय मिद मादौ तव मनो
निधायैके नित्ये निरवधि महाभोग रसिकाः ।
भजन्ति त्वां चिन्तामणि गुणनिबद्धाक्ष वलयाः
शिवाग्नौ जुह्वन्तः सुरभिघृत धाराहुति शतैः ॥ ३३

शरीरं त्वं शम्भोः शशि मिहिर वक्षोरुह युगं
तवात्मानं मन्ये भगवति नवात्मान मनघम् ।
अतः शेषः शेषीत्यय मुभय साधारणतया
स्थितः सम्बन्धो वां समरस परानन्द परयोः ॥ ३४

मनस्त्वं व्योम त्वं मरुदसि मरुत्सारथि रसि
त्वमाप स्त्वं भूमि स्त्वयि परिणतायां न हि परम् ।
त्वमेव स्वात्मानं परिणमयितुं विश्व वपुषा
चिदानन्दाकारं शिवयुवति भावेन बिभृषे ॥ ३५

तवाज्ञचक्रस्थं तपन शशि कोटि द्युतिधरं
परं शंभुं वन्दे परिमिलित पार्श्व परचिता ।
यमाराध्यन् भक्त्या रवि शशि शुचीना मविषये
निरालोके ऽलोके निवसति हि भालोक भुवने ॥ 36

विशुद्धौ ते शुद्धस्फटिक विशदं व्योम जनकं
शिवं सेवे देवीमपि शिवसमान व्यवसिताम् ।
ययो: कांत्या यांत्या: शशिकिरण् सारूप्यसरणे:
विधूतान्त ध्र्वान्ता विलसति चकोरीव जगती ॥ 37

समुन्मीलत् संवित्कमल मकरन्दैक रसिकं
भजे हंसद्वन्द्वं किमपि महतां मानसचरम् ।
यदालापात् अष्टादश गुणित विद्यापरिणति:
यदादत्ते दोषात् गुण मखिल मद्भ्यः पय इव ॥ 38

तव स्वाधिष्ठाने हुतवह मधिष्ठाय निरतं
तमीडे संवर्तं जननि महतीं तां च समयाम् ।
यदालोके लोकान् दहति महसि क्रोध कलिते
दयार्द्रा या दृष्टिः शिशिर मुपचारं रचयति ॥ 39

तटित्वन्तं शक्त्या तिमिर परिपन्थि स्फुरणया
स्फुर न्ना नारत्नाभरण परिणद्धेन्द्र धनुषम् ।
तव श्यामं मेघं कमपि मणिपूरैक शरणं
निषेवे वर्षन्तं हरमिहिर तप्तं त्रिभुवनम् ॥ 40

तवाधारे मूले सह समयया लास्यपरया
नवात्मानं मन्ये नवरस महाताण्डव नटम् ।
उभाभ्या मेताभ्या मुदय विधि मुद्दिश्य दयया
सनाथाभ्यां जज्ञे जनक जननीमज्जगदिदम् ॥ 41

द्वितीय भागः – सौन्दर्य लहरी

गतै र्माणिक्यत्वं गगनमणिभिः सान्द्रघटितं
किरीटं ते हैमं हिमगिरिसुते कीर्तयति यः ॥
स नीडेयच्छाया च्छुरण शबलं चन्द्र शकलं
धनुः शौनासीरं किमिति न निबध्नाति धिषणाम् ॥ 42

धुनोतु ध्वान्तं न स्तुलित दलितेन्दीवर वनं
घनस्निग्ध श्लक्ष्णं चिकुर निकुरुम्बं तव शिवे ।
यदीयं सौरभ्यं सहज मुपलब्धं सुमनसो
वसन्त्यस्मिन् मन्ये वलमथन वाटी विटपिनाम् ॥ 43

तनोतु क्षेमं न स्तव वदनसौन्दर्यलहरी
परीवाहस्त्रोतः सरणिरिव सीमन्तसरणिः।
वहन्ती सिन्दूरं प्रबलकबरी भार तिमिर
द्विषां बृन्दै र्वन्दीकृतमिव नवीनार्क किरणम् ॥ 44

अरालै स्वाभाव्या दलिकलभ सश्रीभि रलकैः
परीतं ते वक्त्रं परिहसति पङ्केरुहरुचिम् ।
दरस्मेरे यस्मिन् दशनरुचि किञ्जल्क रुचिरे
सुगन्धौ माद्यन्ति स्मरदहन चक्षु र्मधुलिहः ॥ 45

ललाटं लावण्य द्युति विमल माभाति तव यत्
द्वितीयं तन्मन्ये मकुटघटितं चन्द्रशकलम् ।
विपर्यास न्यासा दुभयमपि सम्भूय च मिथः
सुधालेपस्यूतिः परिणमति राका हिमकरः ॥ 46

भ्रुवौ भुग्ने किञ्चिद्भुवन भय भङ्गव्यसनिनि
त्वदीये नेत्राभ्यां मधुकर रुचिभ्यां धृतगुणम् ।
धनु र्मन्ये सव्येतरकर गृहीतं रतिपतेः
प्रकोष्ठे मुष्टौ च स्थगयति निगूढान्तर मुमे ॥ 47

अहः सूते सव्यं तव नयन मर्कात्मकतया
त्रियामां वामं ते सृजति रजनीनायकतया ।
तृतीया ते दृष्टि र्दरदलित हेमाम्बुज रुचिः
समाधत्ते सन्ध्यां दिवसर् निशयो रन्तरचरीम् ॥ 48

विशाला कल्याणी स्फुटरुचि रयोध्या कुवलयैः
कृपाधाराधारा किमपि मधुराऽभोगवतिका ।
अवन्ती दृष्टिस्ते बहुनगर विस्तार विजया
ध्रुवं तत्तन्नाम व्यवहरण योग्याविजयते ॥ 49

कवीनां सन्दर्भ स्तबक मकरन्दैक रसिकं
कटाक्ष व्याक्षेप भ्रमरकलभौ कर्णयुगलम् ।
अमुञ्च्न्तौ दृष्ट्वा तव नवरसास्वाद तरलौ
असूया संसर्गा तलिकनयनं किञ्चिदरुणम् ॥ 50

शिवे शृङ्गारार्द्रा तदितरजने कुत्सनपरा
सरोषा गङ्गायां गिरिशचरिते विस्मयवती ।
हराहिभ्यो भीता सरसिरुह सौभाग्य जननी
सखीषु स्मेरा ते मयि जननि दृष्टिः सकरुणा ॥ 51

गते कर्णाभ्यर्णं गरुत इव पक्ष्माणि दधती
पुरां भेत्तु श्चित्तप्रशम रस विद्रावण फले ।
इमे नेत्रे गोत्राधरपति कुलोत्तं सकलिके
तवाकर्णाकृष्ट स्मरशर विलासं कलयतः ॥ 52

विभक्त त्रैवर्ण्यं व्यतिकरित लीलाञ्जनतया
विभाति त्वन्नेत्र त्रितय मिद मीशानदयिते ।
पुनः स्रष्टुं देवान् द्रुहिण हरि रुद्रानुपरतान्
रजः सत्वं बिभ्रत् तम इति गुणानां त्रयमिव ॥ 53

पवित्रीकर्तुं नः पशुपति पराधीन हृदये
दयामित्रै नेत्रै ररुण धवल श्याम रुचिभिः ।
नदः शोणो गङ्गा तपनतनयेति ध्रुवममुम्
त्रयाणां तीर्थाना मुपनयसि सम्भेद मनघम् ॥ 54

निमेषोन्मेषाभ्यां प्रलयमुदयं याति जगति
तवेत्याहुः सन्तो धरणिधर राजन्यतनये ।
त्वदुन्मेषाज्जातं जगदिद मशेषं प्रलयतः
परेत्रातुं शंङ्गे परिहृत निमेषा स्तव दृशः ॥ 55

तवापर्णे कर्णे जपनयन पैशुन्य चकिता
निलीयन्ते तोये नियत मनिमेषाः शफरिकाः ।
इयं च श्री बर्द्धच्छदपुटकवाटं कुवलयं
जहाति प्रत्यूषे निशि च विघटय्य प्रविशति ॥ 56

दृशा द्राघीयस्या दरदलित नीलोत्पल रुचा
दवीयांसं दीनं स्नपय कृपया मामपि शिवे ।
अनेनायं धन्यो भवति न च ते हानिरियता
वने वा हर्म्ये वा समकर निपातो हिमकरः ॥ 57

अरालं ते पालीयुगल मगराजन्यतनये
न केषा माधत्ते कुसुमशर कोदण्ड कुतुकम् ।
तिरश्चीनो यत्र श्रवणपथ मुल्लङ्घ्य विलसन्
अपाङ्ग व्यासङ्गो दिशति शरसन्धान धिषणाम् ॥ 58

स्फुरद्गण्डाभोग प्रतिफलित ताटङ्कयुगलं
चतुश्चक्रं मन्ये तव मुखमिदं मन्मथरथम् ।
यमारुह्य द्रुह्य त्यवनिरथ मर्केन्दुचरणं
महावीरो मारः प्रमथपतये सज्जितवते ॥ 59

सरस्वत्याः सूक्ती रमृतलहरी कौशलहरीः
पिब्नत्याः शर्वाणि श्रवण चुलुकाभ्या मविरलम् ।
चमत्कार श्लाघाचलित शिरसः कुण्डलगणो
झणत्कारैस्तारैः प्रतिवचन माचष्ट इव ते ॥ 60

असौ नासावंश स्तुहिनगिरिवंश ध्वजपटि
त्वदीयो नेदीयः फलतु फल मस्माकमुचितम् ।
वहत्यन्तर्मुक्ताः शिशिरकर निश्वास गलितं
समृद्ध्या यत्तासां बहिरपि च मुक्तामणिधरः ॥ 61

प्रकृत्या रक्ताया स्तव सुदति दन्तच्छदरुचेः
प्रवक्ष्ये सादृश्यं जनयतु फलं विद्रुमलता ।
न बिंबं तद्बिम्ब प्रतिफलन रागा दरुणितं
तुलामध्यारोढुं कथमिव विलज्जेत कलया ॥ 62

स्मितज्योत्स्नाजालं तव वदनचन्द्रस्य पिबतां
चकोराणा मासी दतिरसतया चञ्चु जडिमा ।
अतस्ते शीतांशो रमृतलहरी माम्लरुचयः
पिबन्ती स्वच्छन्दं निशि निशि भृशं काञ्जि कधिया ॥ 63

अविश्रान्तं पत्युर्गुणगण कथाम्रेडनजपा
जपापुष्पच्छाया तव जननि जिह्वा जयति सा ।
यदग्रासीनायाः स्फटिकदृष दच्छच्छविमयि
सरस्वत्या मूर्तिः परिणमति माणिक्यवपुषा ॥ 64

रणे जित्वा दैत्या नपहृत शिरस्त्रैः कवचिभिः
निवृत्तै श्रण्डांश त्रिपुरहर निर्माल्य विमुखैः ।
विशाखेन्द्रोपेन्द्रैः शशिविशद कर्पूरशकला
विलीयन्ते मातस्तव वदनताम्बूल कबलाः ॥ 65

विपञ्च्या गायन्ती विविध मपदानं पशुपते
स्त्वयारब्धे वक्तुं चलितशिरसा साधुवचने ।
तदीयैं र्माधुयैं रपलपित तन्त्रीकलरवां
निजां वीणां वाणी निचुलयति चोलेन निभृतम् ॥ 66

कराग्रेण स्पृष्टं तुहिनगिरिणा वत्सलतया
गिरिशेनो दस्तं मुहुरधरपानाकुलतया ।
करग्राह्यं शम्भोर्मुखमुकुरवृन्तं गिरिसुते
कथंकारं ब्रूम स्तव चुबुकमोपम्यरहितम् ॥ 67

भुजाश्रेषान्नित्यं पुरदमयितुः कण्डकवती
तव ग्रीवा धत्ते मुखकमलनाल श्रियमियम् ।
स्वतः श्वेता काला गरु बहुल जम्बालमलिना
मृणालीलालित्यं वहति यदधो हारलतिका ॥ 68

गले रेखास्तिस्रो गति गमक गीतैक निपुणे
विवाह व्यानद्ध प्रगुणगुण सङ्ख्या प्रतिभुवः ।
विराजन्ते नानाविध मधुर रागाकर भुवां
त्रयाणां ग्रामाणां स्थिति नियम सीमान इव ते ॥ 69

मृणाली मृद्वीनां तव भुजलतानां चतसृणां
चतुर्भिः सौन्दर्य सरसिजभवः स्तौति वदनैः ।
नखेभ्यः सन्त्रस्यन् प्रथम मथना दन्तकरिपोः
चतुर्णां शीर्षाणां सम मभयहस्तार्पण धिया ॥ 70

नखाना मुद्योतै र्नवनलिनरागं विहसतां
कराणां ते कान्तिं कथय कथयामः कथमुमे ।
कयाचिद्वा साम्यं भजतु कलया हन्त कमलं
यदि क्रीडल्लक्ष्मी चरणतल लाक्षारस चणम् ॥ 71

समं देवि स्कन्द द्विपवदन पीतं स्तनयुगं
तवेदं नः खेदं हरतु सततं प्रस्नुत मुखम् ।
यदालोक्याशङ्काकुलित हृदयो हासजनकः
स्वकुम्भौ हेरम्बः परिमृशति हस्तेन झटिति ॥ 72

अमू ते वक्षोजौ अमृतरस माणिक्य कुतुपौ
न सन्देहस्पन्दो नगपति पताके मनसि नः ।
पिबन्तौ तौ यस्मा दविदित वधूसङ्ग रसिकौ
कुमारावद्यापि द्विरदवदन क्रौञ्चदलनौ ॥ 73

वहत्यम्ब स्तंबेरम दनुज कुम्भप्रकृतिभिः
समारब्धां मुक्तामणिभिरमलां हारलतिकाम् ।
कुचाभोगो बिम्बाधर रुचिभि रन्तः शबलितां
प्रताप व्यामिश्रां पुरदमयितुः कीर्तिमिव ते ॥ 74

तव स्तन्यं मन्ये धरणिधरकन्ये हृदयतः
पयः पारावारः परिवहति सारस्वतमिव ।
दयावत्या दत्तं द्रविडशिशु आस्वाद्य तव यत्
कवीनां प्रौढाना मजनि कमनीयः कवयिता ॥ 75

हरक्रोध ज्वालावलिभि रवलीढेन वपुषा
गभीरे ते नाभीसरसि कृतसङ्गो मनसिजः ।
समुत्तस्थौ तस्मा दचलतनये धूमलतिका
जनस्तां जानीते तव जननि रोमावलिरिति ॥ 76

यदेतत्कालिन्दी तनुतर तरङ्गाकृति शिवे
कृशे मध्ये किञ्चिज्जननि तव यद्भाति सुधियाम् ।
विमर्दा दन्योन्यं कुचकलशयो रन्तरगतं
तनूभूतं व्योम प्रविशदिव नाभिं कुहरिणीम् ॥ 77

स्थिरो गङ्गा वर्तः स्तनमुकुल रोमावलि लता
कलावालं कुण्डं कुसुमशर तेजो हुतभुजः ।
रते र्लीलागारं किमपि तव नाभिर्गिरिसुते
बेलद्वारं सिद्धे गिरिशनयनानां विजयते ॥ 78

निसर्ग क्षीणस्य स्तनतट भरेण क्लमजुषो
नमन्मूर्ते र्नरीतिलक शनकै त्रुट्यत इव ।
चिरं ते मध्यस्य त्रुटित तटिनी तीर तरुणा
समावस्था स्थेम्नो भवतु कुशलं शैलतनये ॥ 79

कुचौ सद्यः स्विद्य त्तटघटित कूर्पासभिदुरौ
कषन्तौ दोर्मूले कनककलशाभौ कलयता ।
तव त्रातुं भङ्गादलमिति वलग्नं तनुभुवा
त्रिधा नद्धं देवी त्रिवलि लवलीवल्लिभिरिव ॥ 80

गुरुत्वं विस्तारं क्षितिधरपतिः पार्वति निजात्
नितम्बा दाच्छिद्य त्वयि हरण रूपेण निदधे ।
अतस्ते विस्तीर्णो गुरुरयमशेषां वसुमतीं
नितम्ब प्राग्भारः स्थगयति लघुत्वं नयति च ॥ 81

करीन्द्राणां शुण्डान् कनककदली काण्डपटलीं
उभाभ्यामूरुभ्या मुभयमपि निर्जित्य भवति ।
सुवृत्ताभ्यां पत्युः प्रणतिकठिनाभ्यां गिरिसुते
विधिज्ञे जानुभ्यां विबुध करिकुम्भ द्वयमसि ॥ 82

पराजेतुं रुद्रं द्विगुणशरगर्भौ गिरिसुते
निषङ्गौ जङ्घे ते विषमविशिखो बाढ मकृत ।
यदग्रे दृश्यन्ते दशशरफलाः पादयुगली
नखाग्रच्छन्मानः सुर मकुट शाणैक निशिताः ॥ 83

श्रुतीनां मूर्धानो दधति तव यौ शेखरतया
ममाप्येतौ मातः शिरसि दयया देहि चरणौ ।
ययो: पाद्यं पाथः पशुपति जटाजूट तटिनी
ययो र्लाक्षा लक्ष्मी ररुण हरिचूडामणि रुचिः ॥ 84

नमो वाकं ब्रूमो नयन रमणीयाय पदयोः
तवास्मै द्वन्द्वाय स्फुट रुचि रसालक्तकवते ।
असूयत्यत्यन्तं यदभिहननाय स्पृहयते
पशूना मीशानः प्रमदवन कङ्केलितरवे ॥ 85

मृषा कृत्वा गोत्रस्खलन मथ वैलक्ष्यनमितं
ललाटे भर्तारं चरणकमले ताडयति ते ।
चिरादन्तः शल्यं दहनकृत मुन्मूलितवता
तुलाकोटिक्वाणैः किलिकिलित मीशान रिपुणा ॥ 86

हिमानी हन्तव्यं हिमगिरिनिवासैक चतुरौ
निशायां निद्राणं निशि चरमभागे च विशदौ ।
वरं लक्ष्मीपात्रं श्रिय मतिसृजन्तौ समयिनां
सरोजं त्वत्पादौ जननि जयत श्चित्रमिह किम् ॥ 87

पदं ते कीर्तीनां प्रपदमपदं देवि विपदां
कथं नीतं सद्भिः कठिन कमठी कर्पर तुलाम् ।
कथं वा बाहुभ्या मुपयमनकाले पुरभिदा
यदादाय न्यस्तं दृषदि दयमानेन मनसा ॥ 88

नखै र्नाकस्त्रीणां करकमल सङ्कोच शशिभिः
तरूणां दिव्यानां हसत इव ते चण्डि चरणौ ।
फलानि स्वःस्थेभ्यः किसलय कराग्रेण ददतां
दरिद्रेभ्यो भद्रां श्रियमनिश मह्णाय ददतौ ॥ 89

ददाने दीनेभ्यः श्रियमनिश माशानुसदृशीं
अमन्दं सौन्दर्यं प्रकर मकरन्दं विकिरति ।
तवास्मिन् मन्दार स्तबक सुभगे यातु चरणे
निमज्जन् मज्जीवः करणचरणः षट्चरणताम् ॥ 90

पदन्यास क्रीडा परिचय मिवारब्धु मनसः
स्खलन्तस्ते खेलं भवनकलहंसा न जहति ।
अतस्तेषां शिक्षां सुभगमणि मञ्जीर रणित
च्छलादाचक्षाणं चरणकमलं चारुचरिते ॥ 91

गतास्ते मञ्चत्वं द्रुहिण हरि रुद्रेश्वर भृतः
शिवः स्वच्छ च्छाया घटित कपट प्रच्छदपटः ।
त्वदीयानां भासां प्रतिफलन रागारुणतया
शरीरी श्रृङ्गारो रस इव दृशां दोग्धि कुतुकम् ॥ 92

अराला केशेषु प्रकृति सरला मन्दहसिते
शिरीषाभा चित्ते दृषदुपलशोभा कुचतटे ।
भृशं तन्वी मध्ये पृथु रुरसिजारोह विषये
जगत्रातुं शम्भो जयति करुणा काचिदरुणा ॥ 93

कलङ्कः कस्तूरी रजनिकर बिम्बं जलमयं
कलाभिः कपूरै र्मरकतकरण्डं निबिडितम् ।
अतस्त्वद्भोगेन प्रतिदिनमिदं रिक्तकुहरं
विधि भूयो भूयो निबिडयति नूनं तव कृते ॥ 94

पुराराते रन्तः पुरमसि तत स्त्वच्चरणयोः
सपर्या मर्यादा तरलकरणाना मसुलभा ।
तथा ह्येते नीताः शतमखमुखाः सिद्धिमतुलां
तव द्वारोपान्तः स्थितिभि रणिमाद्याभि रमराः ॥ 95

कलत्रं वैधात्रं कतिकति भजन्ते न कवयः
श्रियो देव्याः को वा न भवति पतिः कैरपि धनैः ।
महादेवं हित्वा तव सति सतीना मचरमे
कुचाभ्या मासङ्गः कुरवक तरो रप्यसुलभः ॥ 96

गिरामाहु देवीं द्रुहिणगृहिणी मागमविदो
हरेः पत्नीं पद्मां हरसहचरी मद्रितनयाम् ।
तुरीया कापि त्वं दुरधिगम निस्सीम महिमा
महामाया विश्वं भ्रमयसि परब्रह्ममहिषि ॥ 97

कदा काले मातः कथय कलितालक्तककरसं
पिबेयं विद्यार्थी तव चरण निर्णेजनजलम् ।
प्रकृत्या मूकानामपि च कविता०कारणतया
कदा धत्ते वाणीमुखकमल ताम्बूल रसताम् ॥ 98

सरस्वत्या लक्ष्म्या विधि हरि सपत्नो विहरते
रतेः पातिव्रत्यं शिथिलयति रम्येण वपुषा ।
चिरं जीवन्नेव क्षपित पशुपाश व्यतिकरः
परानन्दाभिख्यं रसयति रसं त्वद्भजनवान् ॥ 99

प्रदीप ज्वालाभि दिवसकर नीराजनविधिः
सुधासूते श्रन्द्रोपल जललवै रघ्यरचना ।
स्वकीयैरम्भोभिः सलिल निधि सौहित्यकरणं
त्वदीयाभि र्वाग्भि स्तव जननि वाचां स्तुतिरियम् ॥ 100

फलश्रुति

सौन्दयलहरि मुख्यस्तोत्रं संवार्तदायकम् ।
भगवद्पाद सन्क्लुप्तं पठेन् मुक्तौ भवेन्नरः ॥

॥ सौन्दर्यलहरि स्तोत्रं सम्पूर्णं ॥

*****

Soundaryalahari – Verses – English

Prathama Bhāgaḥ – First Part – Ānanda Lahari

Bhumauskhalita Pādānām Bhūmirēvā Valambanam |
Tvayī Jātā Parādhānām Tvamēva Śaraṇam Śivē ||

Śivaḥ Śaktyā Yuktō Yadi Bhavati Śaktaḥ Prabhavituṃ
Na Chēdēvaṃ Dēvō Na Khalu Kuśalaḥ Spanditumapi |
Atastvām Ārādhyāṃ Hari Hara Viriñcādibhi Rapi
Praṇantuṃ Stōtuṃ Vā Katha Makrta Puṇyaḥ Prabhavati || 1

Tanīyāṃsuṃ Pāṃsuṃ Tava Charaṇa Paṅkēruha Bhavaṃ
Viriñchiḥ Sañchinvan Virachayati Lōkā Navikalam |
Vahatyēnaṃ Śauriḥ Kathamapi Sahasrēṇa Śirasāṃ
Haraḥ Saṅkṣud Yainaṃ Bhajati Bhasitōddhūḻa Navidhim || 2

Avidyānā Manta Stimira Mihira Dvīpanagarī
Jaḍānāṃ Chaitanya Stabaka Makaranda Śrutijharī |
Daridrāṇāṃ Chintāmaṇi Guṇanikā Janmajaladhau
Nimagnānāṃ Daṃṣṭrā Muraripu Varāhasya Bhavati || 3

Tvadanyaḥ Pāṇibhyāmabhayavaradō Daivatagaṇaḥ
Tvamēkā Naivāsi Prakaṭita Varābhītyabhinayā |
Bhayāt Trātuṃ Dātuṃ Phalamapi Cha Vāñchāsamadhikaṃ
Śaraṇyē Lōkānāṃ Tava Hi Charaṇāvēva Nipuṇau || 4

Haristvāmāradhya Praṇata Jana Saubhāgya Jananīṃ
Purā Nārī Bhūtvā Puraripumapi Kṣōbha Manayat |
Smarō'pi Tvāṃ Natvā Ratinayana Lēhyēna Vapuṣā
Munīnāmapyantaḥ Prabhavati Hi Mōhāya Mahatām || 5

Dhanuḥ Pauṣpaṃ Maurvī Madhukaramayī Pañcha Viśikhāḥ
Vasantaḥ Sāmantō Malayamarudāyōdhana Rathaḥ |
Tathāpyēkaḥ Sarvaṃ Himagirisutē Kāmapi Kṛpāṃ
Apāṅgāttē Labdhvā Jagadida Manaṅgō Vijayatē || 6

Kvaṇatkāñchī Dāmā Kari Kalabha Kumbha Stananatā
Parikṣīṇā Madhyē Pariṇata Śarachchandra Vadanā |
Dhanurbāṇān Pāśaṃ Sṛṇimapi Dadhānā Karatalaiḥ
Purastā Dāstāṃ Naḥ Puramathitu Rāhō Puruṣikā || 7

Sudhāsindhōrmadhyē Suraviṭa Pivāṭī Parivṛtē
Maṇidvīpē Nīpō Pavanavati Chintāmaṇi Gṛhē |
Śivākārē Mañchē Paramaśiva Paryaṅka Nilayām
Bhajanti Tvāṃ Dhanyāḥ Katichana Chidānanda Laharīm || 8

Mahīṃ Mūlādhārē Kamapi Maṇipūrē Hutavahaṃ
Sthitaṃ Svadhiṣṭānē Hṛdi Maruta Mākāśa Mupari |
Manō'pi Bhrūmadhyē Sakalamapi Bhitvā Kulapathaṃ
Sahasrārē Padmē Sa Harahasi Patyā Viharasē || 9

Sudhādhārāsārai Ścharaṇayugalānta Rvigalitaiḥ
Prapañchaṃ Siñcantī Punarapi Rasāmnāya Mahasaḥ |
Avāpya Svāṃ Bhūmiṃ Bhujaganibha Madhyuṣṭha Valayaṃ
Sva Mātmānaṃ Kṛtvā Svapiṣi Kulakuṇḍē Kuhariṇi || 10

Chaturbhiḥ Śrīkaṇthaiḥ Śivayuvatibhiḥ Pañchabhirapi
Prabhinnābhiḥ Śambhōrnavabhirapi Mūlaprakṛtibhiḥ |
Chatuśchatvāriṃśad Vasudala Kalāśch Trivalaya
Trirēkhābhiḥ Sārdhaṃ Tava Śaraṇakōṇāḥ Pariṇatāḥ || 11

Tvadīyaṃ Soundaryaṃ Tuhinagirikanyē Tulayituṃ
Kavīndrāḥ Kalpantē Kathamapi Viriñchi Prabhṛtayaḥ |
Yadālōkautsukyā Damaralalanā Yānti Manasā
Tapōbhirduṣprāpāmapi Giriśa Sāyujya Padavīm || 12

Naraṃ Varṣīyāṃsaṃ Nayanavirasaṃ Narmasu Jaḍaṃ
Tavāpāṅgālōkē Patita Manudhāvanti Śataśaḥ |
Galadvēṇībandhāḥ Kuchakalaśa Vistrista Sichayā
Haṭhāt Truṭyatkāñyō Vigalita Dukūlā Yuvatayaḥ || 13

Kṣitau Ṣaṭpañchāśad Dvisamadhika Pañchāśa Dudakē
Hutāśē Dvāṣaṣṭi Śchaturadhika Pañchāśa Danilē |
Divi Dviḥ Ṣaṭ Trimśat Manasi Cha Chatuḥṣaṣṭiriti Yē
Mayūkhā Stēṣā Mapyupari Tava Pādāmbuja Yugam || 14

Śarajjyōtsnā Śuddhāṃ Śaśiyuta Jaṭājūṭa Makuṭāṃ
Vara Trāsa Trāṇa Sphaṭikaghaṭikā Pustaka Karām |
Sakṛnna Tvā Natvā Kathamiva Satāṃ Sannidadhatē
Madhu Kṣīra Drākṣā Madhurima Dhurīṇāḥ Phaṇitayaḥ ‖ 15

Kavīndrāṇāṃ Chētaḥ Kamalavana Bālātapa Ruchiṃ
Bhajantē Yē Santaḥ Katichidaruṇāmēva Bhavatīm |
Viriñchi Prēyasyā Staruṇatara Śṛṅgāra Laharī
Gabhīrābhi Rvāgbhiḥ Rvidadhati Satāṃ Rañjanamamī ‖ 16

Savitrībhi Rvāchāṃ Chaśi Maṇi Śilā Bhaṅga Ruchibhi
Rvaśinyadyābhi Stvāṃ Saha Janani Sañchintayati Yaḥ |
Sa Kartā Kāvyānāṃ Bhavati Mahatāṃ Bhaṅgiruchibhi
Rvachōbhi Rvāgdēvī Vadana Kamalāmōda Madhuraiḥ ‖ 17

Tanuchchāyābhistē Taruṇa Taraṇi Śrīsaraṇibhi
Rdivaṃ Sarvā Murvī Maruṇima Nimagnāṃ Smarati Yaḥ |
Bhavantyasya Trasya Dvanahariṇa Śālīna Nayanāḥ
Sahōrvaśyā Vaśyāḥ Kati Kati Na Gīrvāṇa Gaṇikāḥ ‖ 18

Mukhaṃ Binduṃ Kṛtvā Kuchayugamadha Stasya Tadadhō
Harārdhaṃ Dhyāyēdyō Haramahiṣi Tē Manmathakalām |
Sa Sadyaḥ Saṅkṣōbhaṃ Nayati Vanitā Ityatilaghu
Trilōkīmapyāśu Bhramayati Ravīndu Stanayugām ‖ 19

Kirantī Maṅgēbhyaḥ Kiraṇa Nikurumbāmṛtarasaṃ
Hṛdi Tvā Mādhattē Himakaraśilā Mūrtimiva Yaḥ |
Sa Sarpāṇāṃ Darpaṃ Śamayati Śakuntādhipa Iva
Jvarapluṣṭān Dṛṣṭyā Sukhayati Sudhādhārasirayā ‖ 20

Taṭillēkhā Tanvīṃ Tapana Śaśi Vaiśvānara Mayīṃ
Niṣaṇṇāṃ Ṣaṇṇāmapyupari Kamalānāṃ Tava Kalāṃ |
Mahāpadmāṭavyāṃ Mṛdita Malamāyēna Manasā
Mahāntaḥ Paśyantō Dadhati Paramāhlāda Laharīm ‖ 21

Bhavāni Tvaṃ Dāsē Mayi Vitara Dṛṣṭiṃ Sakaruṇāṃ
Iti Stōtuṃ Vāñchan Kathayati Bhavāni Tvamiti Yaḥ |
Tadaiva Tvaṃ Tasmai Diśasi Nijasāyujya Padavīṃ
Mukunda Brahmēndra Sphuṭa Makuṭa Nīrājitapadām ‖ 22

Tvayā Hṛtvā Vāmaṃ Vapu Raparitṛptēna Manasā
Śarīrārdhaṃ Śambhōḥ Aparamapi Śaṅkē Hṛtamabhūt |
Yadētat Tvadrūpaṃ Sakalamaruṇābhaṃ Trinayanaṃ
Kuchābhyāmānamraṃ Kuṭila Śaśichūḍāla Makuṭam || 23

Jagatsūtē Dhātā Hariravati Rudraḥ Kṣapayatē
Tiraskurva Nnētat Svamapi Vapu Rīśa Stirayati |
Sadā Pūrvaḥ Sarvaṃ Tadida Manugrhṇāti Cha Śiva
Stavājjñām Ālambya Kṣaṇachalitayō Rbhrūlatikayōḥ || 24

Trayāṇāṃ Dēvānāṃ Triguṇa Janitānāṃ Tava Śivē
Bhavēt Pūjā Pūjā Tava Charaṇayō Ryā Virachitā |
Tathā Hi Tvatpādōdvahana Maṇipīṭhasya Nikaṭē
Sthitā Hyētē Śaśvanmukulita Karōttaṃsa Makuṭhāḥ || 25

Viriñchiḥ Pañchatvaṃ Vrajati Harirāpnōti Viratiṃ
Vināśaṃ Kīnāśō Bhajati Dhanadō Yāti Nidhanam |
Vitandrī Māhēndrī Vitatirapi Sammīlita Dṛśā
Mahāsaṃhārē'smin Viharati Sati Tvatpati Rasau || 26

Japō Jalpaḥ Śilpaṃ Sakalamapi Mudrāvirachanā
Gatiḥ Prādakṣiṇya Kramaṇa Maśanādyāhuti Vidhiḥ |
Praṇāmaḥ Saṃvēśaḥ Sukhamakhila Mātmārpaṇa Dṛśā
Saparyā Paryāya Stava Bhavatu Yanmē Vilasitam || 27

Sudhāmapyāsvādya Prati Bhaya Jarāmṛtyu Hariṇīṃ
Vipadyantē Viśvē Vidhi Śatamakhādyā Diviṣadaḥ |
Karālaṃ Yat Kṣvēlaṃ Kabalitavataḥ Kālakalanā
Na Śambhōstanmūlaṃ Tava Janani Tāṭaṅka Mahimā || 28

Kirīṭaṃ Vairiñchaṃ Parihara Puraḥ Kaiṭabhabhidaḥ
Kaṭhōrē Kōṭīrē Skalasi Jahi Jambhāri Makuṭam |
Praṇamrēṣvētēṣu Prasabha Mupayātasya Bhavanaṃ
Bhavasyābhyutthānē Tava Parijanōkti Rvijayatē || 29

Svadēhōdbhūtābhi Rghṛṇibhi Raṇimādyābhi Rabhitō
Niṣēvyē Nityē Tvā Mahamiti Sadā Bhāvayati Yaḥ |
Kimāścharyaṃ Tasya Trinayana Samṛddhiṃ Tṛṇayatō
Mahāsaṃvartāgni Rvirachayati Nīrājanavidhiṃ || 30

Chatuḥ Ṣaṣṭayā Tantraiḥ Sakala Matisandhāya Bhuvanaṃ
Sthitastattta Siddhi Prasava Paratantraiḥ Paśupatiḥ |
Punastva Nnirbandhā Dakhila Puruṣārthaika Ghaṭanā
Svatantraṃ Tē Tantraṃ Kṣititala Mavātītaradidam || 31

Śivaḥ Śaktiḥ Kāmaḥ Kṣiti Ratha Raviḥ Śītakiraṇaḥ
Smarō Haṃsaḥ Śakra Stadanu Cha Parā Māra Harayaḥ |
Amī Hṛllēkhābhi Stisṛbhi Ravasānēṣu Ghaṭitāḥ
Bhajantē Varṇāstē Tava Janani Nāmāvayavatām || 32

Smaraṃ Yōniṃ Lakṣmīṃ Tritaya Mida Mādau Tava Manō
Rnidhāyaikē Nityē Niravadhi Mahābhōga Rasikāḥ |
Bhajanti Tvāṃ Chintāmaṇi Guṇanibaddhākṣa Valayāḥ
Śivāgnau Juhvantaḥ Surabhighṛta Dhārāhuti Śatai || 33

Śarīraṃ Tvaṃ Śambhōḥ Śaśi Mihira Vakṣōruha Yugaṃ
Tavātmānaṃ Manyē Bhagavati Navātmāna Managham |
Ataḥ Śēṣaḥ Śēṣītyaya Mubhaya Sādhāraṇatayā
Sthitaḥ Sambandhō Vāṃ Samarasa Parānanda Parayōḥ || 34

Manastvaṃ Vyōma Tvaṃ Marudasi Marutsārathi Rasi
Tvamāpa Stvaṃ Bhūmi Stvayi Pariṇatāyāṃ Na Hi Param |
Tvamēva Svātmānaṃ Pariṇamayituṃ Viśva Vapuṣā
Chidānandākāraṃ Śivayuvati Bhāvēna Bibhṛṣē || 35

Tavājjñachakrasthaṃ Tapana Śaśi Kōṭi Dyutidharaṃ
Paraṃ Śambhum Vandē Parimilita Pārśvaṃ Parachitā |
Yamārādhyan Bhaktyā Ravi Śaśi Śuchīnā Maviṣayē
Nirālōkē 'Lōkē Nivasati Hi Bhālōka Bhuvanē || 36

Viśuddhau Tē Śuddhasphaṭika Viśadaṃ Vyōma Janakaṃ
Śivaṃ Sēvē Dēvīmapi Śivasamāna Vyavasitām |
Yayōḥ Kāntyā Yāntyāḥ Śaśikiraṇ Sārūpyasaraṇēḥ
Vidhūtānta Rdhvāntā Vilasati Chakōrīva Jagatī || 37

Samunmīlat Saṃvitkamala Makarandaika Rasikaṃ
Bhajē Haṃsadvandvaṃ Kimapi Mahatāṃ Mānasacharaṃ |
Yadālāpāt Aṣṭādaśa Guṇita Vidyāpariṇatiḥ
Yadādattē Dōṣāt Guṇa Makhila Madbhyaḥ Paya Iva || 38

Tava Svādhiṣṭhānē Hutavaha Madhiṣṭhāya Nirataṃ
Tamīḍē Saṃvartaṃ Janani Mahatīṃ Tāṃ Cha Samayām |
Yadālōkē Lōkān Dahati Mahasi Krōdha Kalitē
Dayārdrā Yā Dṛṣṭiḥ Śiśira Mupachāraṃ Rachayati || 39

Taṭitvantaṃ Śaktyā Timira Paripanthi Sphuraṇayā
Sphura Nnā Nāratnābharaṇa Pariṇaddhēndra Dhanuṣam |
Tava Śyāmaṃ Mēghaṃ Kamapi Maṇipūraika Śaraṇaṃ
Niṣēvē Varṣantaṃ Haramihira Taptaṃ Tribhuvanam || 40

Tavādhārē Mūlē Saha Samayayā Lāsyaparayā
Navātmānam Manyē Navarasa Mahātāṇḍava Naṭam |
Ubhābhyā Mētābhyā Mudaya Vidhi Muddiśya Dayayā
Sanāthābhyāṃ Jajjñē Janaka Jananīmajjagadidam || 41

<u>Dvitīya Bhāgaḥ – Second Part – *Soundarya Laharī*</u>

Gatai Rmāṇikyatvaṃ Gaganamaṇibhiḥ Sāndraghaṭitaṃ
Kirīṭaṃ Tē Haimaṃ Himagirisutē Kīrtayati Yaḥ |
Sa Nīḍēyachchāyā Chchuraṇa Śabalaṃ Chandra Śakalaṃ
Dhanuḥ Śaunāsīraṃ Kimiti Na Nibadhnāti Dhiṣaṇām || 42

Dhunōtu Dhvāntaṃ Na Stulita Daḻitēndīvara Vanaṃ
Ghanasnigdha Ślakṣṇaṃ Chikura Nikurumbaṃ Tava Śivē |
Yadīyaṃ Saurabhyaṃ Sahaja Mupalabdhuṃ Sumanasō
Vasantyasmin Manyē Valamathana Vāṭī Viṭapinām || 43

Tanōtu Kṣēmaṃ Na Stava VadanaSoundaryalaharī
Parīvāhasrōtaḥ Saraṇiriva Sīmantasaraṇiḥ|
Vahantī Sindūraṃ Prabalakabarī Bhāra Timira
Dviṣāṃ Bṛndai Rbandīkṛtamiva Navīnārka Kiraṇam || 44

Arālai Svābhāvyā Dalikalabha Saśrībhi Ralakaiḥ
Parītaṃ Tē Vaktraṃ Parihasati Paṅkēruharuchim |
Darasmērē Yasmin Daśanaruchi Kiñjalka Ruchirē
Sugandhau Mādyanti Smaradahana Chakṣu Rmadhulihaḥ || 45

Lalāṭaṃ Lāvaṇya Dyuti Vimala Mābhāti Tava Yat
Dvitīyaṃ Tanmanyē Makuṭaghaṭitaṃ Chandraśakalam |
Viparyāsa Nyāsā Tubhayamapi Sambhūya Cha Mithaḥ
Sudhālēpasyūtiḥ Pariṇamati Rākā Himakaraḥ || 46

Bhruvau Bhugnē Kiñchidbhuvana Bhaya Bhaṅgavyasanini
Tvadīyē Nētrābhyāṃ Madhukara Ruchibhyāṃ Dhṛtaguṇam I
Dhanu Rmanyē Savyētarakara Gṛhītaṃ Ratipatēḥ
Prakōṣṭē Muṣṭau Cha Sthagayati Nigūḍhāntara Mumē II 47

Ahaḥ Sūtē Savyam Tava Nayana Markātmakatayā
Triyāmāṃ Vāmaṃ Tē Sṛjati Rajanīnāyakatayā I
Tṛtīyā Tē Dṛṣṭi Rdaradalita Hēmāmbuja Ruchiḥ
Samādhattē Sandhyāṃ Divasar Niśayō Rantaracharīm II 48

Viśālā Kalyāṇī Sphuṭaruchi Rayōdhyā Kuvalayaiḥ
Kṛpādhārādhārā Kimapi Madhurā"bhōgavatikā I
Avantī Dṛṣṭistē Bahunagara Vistāra Vijayā
Dhruvaṃ Tattannāma Vyavaharaṇa Yōgyāvijayatē II 49

Kavīnāṃ Sandarbha Stabaka Makarandaika Rasikaṃ
Kaṭākṣa Vyākṣēpa Bhramarakalabhau Karṇayugalam I
Amuñchntau Dṛṣṭvā Tava Navarasāsvāda Taralau
Asūyā Saṃsargā Talikanayanaṃ Kiñchidaruṇam II 50

Śivē Śṛuṅgārārdrā Taditarajanē Kutsanaparā
Sarōṣā Gaṅgāyāṃ Giriśacharitē Vismayavatī I
Harāhibhyō Bhītā Sarasiruha Saubhāgya Jananī
Sakhīṣu Smērā Tē Mayi Janani Dṛṣṭiḥ Sakaruṇā II 51

Gatē Karṇābhyarṇaṃ Garuta Iva Pakṣmāṇi Dadhatī
Purāṃ Bhēttu Śchittapraśama Rasa Vidrāvaṇa Phalē I
Imē Nētrē Gōtrādharapati Kulōttaṃ Sakalikē
Tavākarṇākṛṣṭa Smaraśara Vilāsaṃ KalayataḥII 52

Vibhakta Traivarṇyaṃ Vyatikarita Līlāñjanatayā
Vibhāti Tvannētra Tritaya Mida Mīśānadayitē I
Punaḥ Sraṣṭuṃ Dēvān Druhiṇa Hari Rudrānuparatān
Rajaḥ Satvaṃ Bhibhrat Tama Iti Guṇānāṃ Trayamiva II 53

Pavitrīkartuṃ Naḥ Paśupati Parādhīna Hṛdayē
Dayāmitrai Rnētrai Raruṇa Dhavaḻa Śyāma Ruchibhiḥ I
Nadaḥ Śōṇō Gaṅgā Tapanatanayēti Dhruvamamum
Trayāṇāṃ Tīrthānā Mupanayasi Sambhēda Managham II 54

Nimēṣōnmēṣābhyāṃ Pralayamudayaṃ Yāti Jagati
Tavētyāhuḥ Santō Dharaṇidhara Rājanyatanayē |
Tvadunmēṣājjātaṃ Jagadida Maśēṣaṃ Pralayataḥ
Parētrātuṃ Śaṃṅgē Parihṛta Nimēṣā Stava Dṛṣaḥ || 55

Tavāparṇē Karṇē Japanayana Paiśunya Chakitā
Nilīyantē Tōyē Niyata Manimēṣāḥ Śapharikāḥ |
Iyaṃ Cha Śrī Rbaddhachchada Puṭa Kavāṭaṃ Kuvalayaṃ
Jahāti Pratyūṣē Niśi Cha Vighaṭayya Praviśati || 56

Dṛśā Drāghīyasyā Daradalita Nīlōtpala Ruchā
Davīyāṃsaṃ Dīnaṃ Snapaya Kṛpayā Māmapi Śivē |
Anēnāyaṃ Dhanyō Bhavati Na Cha Tē Hāniriyatā
Vanē Vā Harmyē Vā Samakara Nipātō Himakaraḥ || 57

Arālaṃ Tē Pālīyugala Magarājanyatanayē
Na Kēṣā Mādhattē Kusumaśara Kōdaṇḍa Kutukam |
Tiraśchīnō Yatra Śravaṇapatha Mullaṅghya Vilasan
Apāṅga Vyāsaṅgō Diśati Śarasandhāna Dhiṣaṇām || 58

Sphuradgaṇḍābhōga Pratiphalita Tāṭaṅka Yugalaṃ
Chatuśchakraṃ Manyē Tava Mukhamidaṃ Manmatharatham |
Yamāruhya Druhya Tyavaniratha Markēnducharaṇaṃ
Mahāvīrō Māraḥ Pramathapatayē Sajjitavatē || 59

Sarasvatyāḥ Sūktī Ramṛtalaharī Kauśalaharīḥ
Pibnatyāḥ Śarvāṇi Śravaṇa Chulukābhyā Maviralam |
Chamatkāra Ślāghāchalita Śirasaḥ Kuṇḍalagaṇō
Jhaṇatkāraistāraiḥ Prativachana Māchaṣṭa Iva Tē || 60

Asau Nāsāvaṃśa Stuhinagirivamśa Dhvajapaṭi
Tvadīyō Nēdīyaḥ Phalatu Phala Masmākamuchitam |
Vahatyantarmuktāḥ Śiśirakara Niśvāsa Galitaṃ
Samṛddhyā Yattāsāṃ Bahirapi Cha Muktāmaṇidharaḥ || 61

Prakṛtyā Raktāyā Stava Sudati Dantachchadaruchēḥ
Pravakṣyē Sādṛśyaṃ Janayatu Phalaṃ Vidrumalatā |
Na Bimbaṃ Tadbimba Pratiphalana Rāgā Daruṇitaṃ
Tulāmadhyārōḍhuṃ Kathamiva Vilajjēta Kalayā || 62

Smitajyōtsnājālaṃ Tava Vadanachandrasya Pibatāṃ
Chakōrāṇā Māsī Datirasatayā Chañchu Jaḍimā |
Atastē Śītāṃśō Ramṛtalaharī Māmlaruchayaḥ
Pibantī Svachchandaṃ Niśi Niśi Bhṛśaṃ Kāñji Kadhiyā || 63

Aviśrāntaṃ Patyurguṇagaṇa Kathāmrēḍanajapā
Japāpuṣpachchhāyā Tava Janani Jihvā Jayati Sā |
Yadagrāsīnāyāḥ Sphaṭikadṛṣa Dachchhachchhavimayi
Sarasvatyā Mūrtiḥ Pariṇamati Māṇikyavapuṣā || 64

Raṇē Jitvā Daityā Napahṛta Śirastraiḥ Kavachibhiḥ
Nivṛttai Śchaṇḍāṃśa Tripurahara Nirmālya Vimukhaiḥ |
Viśākhēndrōpēndraiḥ Śaśiviśada Karpūraśakalā
Vilīyantē Mātastava Vadanatāmbūla Kabalāḥ || 65

Vipañchyā Gāyantī Vividha Mapadānaṃ Paśupatē
Stvayārabdhē Vaktuṃ Chalitaśirasā Sādhuvachanē |
Tadīyai Rmādhuryai Rapalapita Tantrīkalaravāṃ
Nijāṃ Vīṇāṃ Vāṇī Nichulayati Chōlēna Nibhṛtam || 66

Karāgrēṇa Spṛṣṭaṃ Tuhinagiriṇā Vatsalatayā
Giriśēnō Dastaṃ Muhuradharapānākulatayā |
Karagrāhyaṃ Śambhōrmukhamukuravṛntaṃ Girisutē
Kathaṅkāraṃ Brūma Stava Chubukamōpamyarahitam || 67

Bhujāślēṣānnityaṃ Puradamayituḥ Kaṇḍakavatī
Tava Grīvā Dhattē Mukhakamalanāla Śriyamiyam |
Svataḥ Śvētā Kālā Garu Bahula Jambālamalinā
Mṛṇālīlālityaṃ Vahati Yadadhō Hāralatikā || 68

Galē Rēkhāstisrō Gati Gamaka Gītaika Nipuṇē
Vivāha Vyānaddha Praguṇaguṇa Saṅkhyā Pratibhuvaḥ |
Virājantē Nānāvidha Madhura Rāgākara Bhuvāṃ
Trayāṇāṃ Grāmāṇāṃ Sthiti Niyama Sīmāna Iva Tē || 69

Mṛṇālī Mṛdvīnāṃ Tava Bhujalatānāṃ Chatasṛṇāṃ
Chaturbhiḥ Soundaryaṃ Sarasijabhavaḥ Stauti Vadanaiḥ |
Nakhēbhyaḥ Santrasyan Prathama Mathanā Dandhakaripōḥ
Chaturṇāṃ Śīrṣāṇāṃ Sama Mabhayahastārpaṇa Dhiyā || 70

Nakhānā Mudyōtai Rnavanalinarāgaṃ Vihasatāṃ
Karāṇāṃ Tē Kāntiṃ Kathaya Kathayāmaḥ Kathamumē |
Kayāchidvā Sāmyaṃ Bhajatu Kalayā Hanta Kamalaṃ
Yadi Krīḍallakṣmī Charaṇatala Lākṣārasa Chaṇam || 71

Samaṃ Dēvi Skanda Dvipavadana Pītaṃ Stanayugaṃ
Tavēdaṃ Naḥ Khēdaṃ Haratu Satataṃ Prasnuta Mukham |
Yadālōkyāśaṅkākulita Hṛdayō Hāsajanakaḥ
Svakumbhau Hērambaḥ Parimṛśati Hastēna Jhaṭiti || 72

Amū Tē Vakṣōjou Amṛtarasa Māṇikya Kutupau
Na Sandēhaspandō Nagapati Patākē Manasi Naḥ |
Pibantau Tau Yasmā Davidita Vadhūsaṅga Rasikau
Kumārāvadyāpi Dviradavadana Krauñchdalanau || 73

Vahatyamba Stambērama Danuja Kumbhaprakṛtibhiḥ
Samārabdhāṃ Muktāmaṇibhiramalāṃ Hāralatikām |
Kuchābhōgō Bimbādhara Ruchibhi Rantaḥ Śabalitāṃ
Pratāpa Vyāmiśrāṃ Puradamayituḥ Kīrtimiva Tē || 74

Tava Stanyaṃ Manyē Dharaṇidharakanyē Hṛdayataḥ
Payaḥ Pārāvāraḥ Parivahati Sārasvatamiva |
Dayāvatyā Dattaṃ Draviḍaśiśu Āsvādya Tava Yat
Kavīnāṃ Prauḍhānā Majani Kamanīyaḥ Kavayitā || 75

Harakrōdha Jvālāvalibhi Ravalīḍhēna Vapuṣā
Gabhīrē Tē Nābhīsarasi Kṛtasaṅgō Manasijaḥ |
Samuttasthau Tasmā Dachalatanayē Dhūmalatikā
Janastāṃ Jānītē Tava Janani Rōmāvaliriti || 76

Yadētatkālindī Tanutara Taraṅgākṛti Śivē
Kṛśē Madhyē Kiñchijjanani Tava Yadbhāti Sudhiyām |
Vimardā Danyōnyaṃ Kuchakalaśayō Rantaragataṃ
Tanūbhūtaṃ Vyōma Praviśadiva Nābhiṃ Kuhariṇīm || 77

Sthirō Gaṅgā Vartaḥ Stanamukula Rōmāvali Latā
Kalāvālaṃ Kuṇḍaṃ Kusumaśara Tējō Hutabhujaḥ |
Ratē Rlīlāgāraṃ Kimapi Tava Nābhirgirisutē
Biladvāraṃ Siddhē Rgiriśanayanānāṃ Vijayatē || 78

Nisarga Kṣīṇasya Stanataṭa Bharēṇa Klamajuṣō
Namanmūrtē Rnārītilaka Śanakai Truṭyata Iva ।
Chiraṃ Tē Madhyasya Truṭita Taṭinī Tīra Taruṇā
Samāvasthā Sthēmnō Bhavatu Kuśalaṃ Śailatanayē ॥ 79

Kuchau Sadyaḥ Svidya Ttaṭaghaṭita Kūrpāsabhidurau
Kaṣantau Dormūlē Kanakakalaśābhau Kalayatā ।
Tava Trātuṃ Bhaṅgādalamiti Valagnaṃ Tanubhuvā
Tridhā Naddham Dēvī Trivali Lavalīvallibhiriva ॥ 80

Gurutvaṃ Vistāraṃ Kṣitidharapatiḥ Pārvati Nijāt
Nitambā Dāchchidya Tvayi Haraṇa Rūpēṇa Nidadhē ।
Atastē Vistīrṇō Gururayamaśēṣāṃ Vasumatīṃ
Nitamba Prāgbhāraḥ Sthagayati Laghutvaṃ Nayati Cha ॥ 81

Karīndrāṇāṃ Śuṇḍān Kanakakadalī Kāṇḍapaṭalīṃ
Ubhābhyāmūrubhyā Mubhayamapi Nirjitya Bhavati ।
Suvṛttābhyāṃ Patyuḥ Praṇatikaṭhinābhyāṃ Girisutē
Vidhijjñē Jānubhyāṃ Vibudha Karikumbha Dvayamasi ॥ 82

Parājētuṃ Rudraṃ Dviguṇaśaragarbhau Girisutē
Niṣaṅgau Jaṅghē Tē Viṣamaviśikhō Bāḍha Makṛta ।
Yadagrē Dṛśyantē Daśaśaraphalāḥ Pādayugalī
Nakhāgrachchanmānaḥ Sura Makuṭa Śāṇaika Niśitāḥ ॥ 83

Śrutīnāṃ Mūrdhānō Dadhati Tava Yau Śēkharatayā
Mamāpyētau Mātaḥ Śirasi Dayayā Dēhi Charaṇau ।
Yayōḥ Pādyaṃ Pāthaḥ Paśupati Jaṭājūṭa Taṭinī
Yayō Rlākṣā Lakṣmī Raruṇa Harichūḍāmaṇi Ruchiḥ ॥ 84

Namō Vākaṃ Brūmō Nayana Ramaṇīyāya Padayōḥ
Tavāsmai Dvandvāya Sphuṭa Ruchi Rasālaktakavatē ।
Asūyatyatyantaṃ Yadabhihananāya Spṛhayatē
Paśūnā Mīśānaḥ Pramadavana Kaṅkēlitaravē ॥ 85

Mṛṣā Kṛtvā Gōtraskhalana Matha Vailakṣyanamitaṃ
Lalāṭē Bhartāraṃ Charaṇakamalē Tāḍayati Tē ।
Chirādantaḥ Śalyaṃ Dahanakṛta Munmūlitavatā
Tulākōṭikvāṇaiḥ Kilikilita Mīśāna Ripuṇā ॥ 86

Himānī Hantavyaṃ Himagirinivāsaika Chaturau
Niśāyāṃ Nidrāṇaṃ Niśi Charamabhāgē Cha Viśadau |
Varaṃ Lakṣmīpātraṃ Śriya Matisṛjantou Samayināṃ
Sarōjaṃ Tvatpādau Janani Jayata Śchitramiha Kim ‖ 87

Padaṃ Tē Kīrtīnāṃ Prapadamapadaṃ Dēvi Vipadāṃ
Kathaṃ Nītaṃ Sadbhiḥ Kaṭhina Kamaṭhī Karpara Tulām |
Kathaṃ Vā Bāhubhyā Mupayamanakālē Purabhidā
Yadādāya Nyastaṃ Dṛṣadi Dayamānēna Manasā ‖ 88

Nakhai Rnākastrīṇāṃ Karakamala Saṅkōcha Śaśibhiḥ
Tarūṇāṃ Divyānāṃ Hasata Iva Tē Chaṇḍi Charaṇau |
Phalāni Svaḥsthēbhyaḥ Kisalaya Karāgrēṇa Dadatāṃ
Daridrēbhyō Bhadrāṃ Śriyamaniśa Mahnāya Dadatau ‖ 89

Dadānē Dīnēbhyaḥ Śriyamaniśa Māśānusadṛśīṃ
Amandaṃ Soundaryaṃ Prakara Makarandaṃ Vikirati |
Tavāsmin Mandāra Stabaka Subhagē Yātu Charaṇē
Nimajjan Majjīvaḥ Karaṇacharaṇaḥ Ṣaṭcharaṇatām ‖ 90

Padanyāsa Krīḍā Parichaya Mivārabdhu Manasaḥ
Skhalantastē Khēlaṃ Bhavanakalahaṃsā Na Jahati |
Atastēṣāṃ Śikṣāṃ Subhagamaṇi Mañjīra Raṇita
Chchalādāchakṣāṇaṃ Charaṇakamalaṃ Chārucharitē ‖ 91

Gatāstē Mañchatvaṃ Druhiṇa Hari Rudrēśvara Bhṛtaḥ
Śivaḥ Svachcha Chchāyā Ghaṭita Kapaṭa Prachchadapaṭaḥ |
Tvadīyānāṃ Bhāsāṃ Pratiphalana Rāgāruṇatayā
Śarīrī Śṛṅgārō Rasa Iva Dṛśāṃ Dōgdhi Kutukam ‖ 92

Arālā Kēśēṣu Prakṛti Saralā Mandahasitē
Śirīṣābhā Chittē Dṛṣadupalaśōbhā Kuchataṭē |
Bhṛśaṃ Tanvī Madhyē Pṛthu Rurasijārōha Viṣayē
Jagattrātuṃ Śambhō Rjayati Karuṇā Kāchidaruṇā ‖ 93

Kalaṅkaḥ Kastūrī Rajanikara Bimbaṃ Jalamayaṃ
Kalābhiḥ Karpūrai Rmarakatakaraṇḍaṃ Nibiḍitam |
Atastvadbhōgēna Pratidinamidaṃ Riktakuharaṃ
Vidhi Rbhūyō Bhūyō Nibiḍayati Nūnaṃ Tava Kṛtē ‖ 94

Purārātē Rantaḥ Puramasi Tata Stvaccaraṇayōḥ
Saparyā Maryādā Taralakaraṇānā Masulabhā |
Tathā Hyētē Nītāḥ Śatamakhamukhāḥ Siddhimatulāṃ
Tava Dvārōpāntaḥ Sthitibhi Raṇimādyābhi Ramarāḥ ǁ 95

Kalatraṃ Vaidhātraṃ Katikati Bhajantē Na Kavayaḥ
Śriyō Dēvyāḥ Kō Vā Na Bhavati Patiḥ Kairapi Dhanaiḥ |
Mahādēvaṃ Hitvā Tava Sati Satīnā Macharamē
Kuchābhyā Māsaṅgaḥ Kuravaka Tarō Rapyasulabhaḥ ǁ 96

Girāmāhu Rdēvīṃ Druhiṇagṛhiṇī Māgamavidō
Harēḥ Patnīṃ Padmāṃ Harasahacharī Madritanayām |
Turīyā Kāpi Tvaṃ Duradhigama Nissīma Mahimā
Mahāmāyā Viśvaṃ Bhramayasi Parabrahmamahiṣi ǁ 97

Kadā Kālē Mātaḥ Kathaya Kalitālaktakarasaṃ
Pibēyaṃ Vidyārthī Tava Charaṇa Nirṇējanajalam |
Prakṛtyā Mūkānāmapi Cha Kavitā0kāraṇatayā
Kadā Dhattē Vāṇīmukhakamala Tāmbūla Rasatām ǁ 98

Sarasvatyā Lakṣmyā Vidhi Hari Sapatnō Viharatē
Ratēḥ Pātivratyaṃ Śithilayati Ramyēṇa Vapuṣā |
Chiraṃ Jīvannēva Kṣapita Paśupāśa Vyatikaraḥ
Parānandābhikhyaṃ Rasayati Rasaṃ Tvadbhajanavān ǁ 99

Pradīpa Jvālābhi Rdivasakara Nīrājanavidhiḥ
Sudhāsūtē Śchandrōpala Jalalavai Raghyarachanā |
Svakīyairambhōbhiḥ Salila Nidhi Sauhityakaraṇaṃ
Tvadīyābhi Rvāgbhi Stava Janani Vāchāṃ Stutiriyam ǁ 100

Soundaryalahari Mukhyastōtraṃ
Saṃvārtadāyakam |
Bhagavadpāda Sankluptaṃ Paṭhēn
Muktau Bhavēnnaraḥ ǁ

Iti Soundaryalahari Stōtraṃ
Sampūrṇaṃ |

*****

About the Author
(http://Ramamurthy.jaagruti.co.in)

Dr. Ramamurthy is a versatile personality having experience and expertise in

various areas of Banking, related IT solutions, Information Security, IT Audit, Vedas, Samskrutam and so on.

His thirst for continuous learning does not subside. Even at the age of late fifties, he did research on an unique topic "Information Technology and Samskrutam" and obtained Ph.D. doctorate degreefrom University of Madras. He is into a project of developing a Samskrutam based compiler.

It is his passion to spread his knowledge and experience through conducting classes, training programmes and writing books.

He has already published books as detailed below. Further books are in pipe line.

#	Title	Remarks	Pages
	Indology Related		
1.	*Shrī Lalita Sahasranāmam*	English translation of Shrī *Bhāskararāya's Bhāṣyam*	750
2.	Power of *Shrī Vidyā*	The secrets demystified – with lucid English rendering and commentaries	80
3.	ஸ்ரீ வித்யையின் ஶக்தி	ஸ்ரீ வித்யா ரகசியங்கள்	100
4.	*Samatā* **समता**	An exposition of Similarities in *Lalita Sahasranāma* with *Soundaryalaharī, Saptaśatī, Viṣṇu Sahasranāma* and *Shrīmad Bhagavad Gīta*	172
5.	ஸமதா – समता	ஸ்ரீ லலிதா ஸஹஸ்ரநாமம் ஸெளந்தர்யலஹரீ, ஸப்தஶதீ, ஸ்ரீ விஷ்ணு ஸஹஸ்ரநாமம் மற்றும் ஸ்ரீமத் பகவத் கீதைகளில் ஒற்றுமையின் ஒரு வெளிப்பாடு	266
6.	*Advaita* in *Shākta*	Advaita Philosophy discussed in Shakta related Books	80
7.	*Shrī Lalitā Triśatī*	300 divine names of the celestial Mother – **English** translation of *Shrī Ādhi Śaṅkara's Bhāṣyam*	193
8.	ஸ்ரீ லலிதா த்ரிஶதி	300 divine names of the celestial Mother – Tamil translation of *Shrī Ādi Śaṅkara's Bhāṣyam*	234
9.	Secrets of *Mahāśakti*	Chandi demystified	78

#	Title	Remarks	Pages
10.	*Daśa Mahā Vidyā*	Ten cosmic forms of the Divine mother	60
11.	ஸ்ரீ வித்யா பேதங்கள்	ஸ்ரீவித்யா உபாசனையின் படிகள் - கோவை ௴தச் சண்டி மலர்	51
12.	*Shrīvidya* Variances	Variances in Srividya Upasana	50
13.	ஸ்ரீ தேவீ ஸ்துதிகள்	பல முக்கிய அம்பாள் ஸ்தோத்ரங்கள்	133
14.	Śrī Devī Stutis – श्री देवी स्तुति:	Various important stotras of Sri Devi	223
15.	ஷண்மத மந்த்ரங்கள்	பொள்ளாச்சி ஸ்ரீ ஸஹஸ்ரசண்டி மஹாயாக நினைவு மலர்	145
16.	*Śanmata Mantras* – षण्मत मन्त्रा:	Important Mantras relating to Gods of six religions	87
17.	தேவதா மந்த்ரங்கள்	அக்கரைப்பட்டி ஸஹஸ்ரசண்டி மஹாயாக நினைவு மலர்	32
18.	ஆதி ௴ங்கரரும் ஷண்மதமும்	ஷண்மதங்களைப் பற்றிய ஒரு அறிமுகம்	32
19.	ஸ்ரீ ஷண்மத தேவதா அர்ச்சனை	ஸ்ரீ மஹா கும்பாபிஷேக மலர்	64
20.	*Vaidhīka* Wedding	Typical Wedding process in English	56
21.	வைதீகத் திருமணம்	Typical Wedding process in Tamil	57
22.	ஸ்ரீகுரு பாத பூஜா விதானம்	சித்தகிரி ஸஹஸ்ரசண்டி மலர்	44
23.	ஸ்ரீவித்யா ௴டாம்னாய மந்த்ரங்கள்	சித்தகிரி ஸஹஸ்ரசண்டி மலர்	60
24.	*Ekatā*	Oneness among Shiva, Vishnu and Shakti	277
25.	ஏகதா एकता	௴வபெருமான், விஷ்ணு மற்றும் ௴க்திக்குள் ஒற்றுமை	300
26.	*Vedas* – An Analytical Perspective	A description of Veda, Vedanta, Vedanga, Jyotisha, Shastra, etc.	240
27.	வேதங்கள் - ஒரு பகுப்பாய்வு	A description of Veda, Vedanta, Vedanga, Jyotisha, Shastra, etc.	280
28.	பரமாச்சார்யாள் நோக்கில் ஸ்ரீ லலிதாம்பிகா	The explanation given by Paramacharya on some of the names in Lalita Sahasranama	175
29.	*Şaṇṇavati Tarpaṇa*	Repaying Debts to Ancestors	42
30.	ஷண்ணவதி தர்பணம்	முன்னோர் கடன் தீர்த்தல்	48
31.	*Shrī Mahā Pratyangirā Devī*	Holy Divine mother in ferocious form	41
32.	ஸ்ரீ மஹா ப்ரத்யங்கிரா தேவீ	தெய்வீக அன்னையின் பயங்கர வடிவம்	51
33.	*Śrī Chakra Navāvarṇam*	Marvels of *Śrī Chakra*	115
34.	ஸ்ரீ சக்ர நவாவர்ணம்	ஸ்ரீ சக்ரத்தின் அதிசயங்கள்	130

#	Title	Remarks	Pages
35.	அம்பிகையின் (திரு) அவதாரங்கள்	ஸ்ரீ தேவியின் பல்வேறு அவதாரங்கள்	142
36.	Incarnations of Holy Mother	Different Incarnations of *Śrī Devī*	140
37.	ஸ்ரீ பிரணவானந்தர் - ஒரு சரிதம்	ஒரு அரிய ஸ்வாமிகளின் திவ்ய சரிதம்	121
38.	ஸன்யாஸம் - ஓர் அலசல்	ஹிந்து மத ஸன்யாஸ பேதங்கள் - ஒரு பகுப்பாய்வு	140
39.	Asceticism – an Analysis	A Study of Hindu *Sanyasam*	140
40.	ஶாந்தமும் ப்ரணவமும்	(**ஸ்ரீ** ஶாந்தானந்தரும் **ஸ்ரீ** ப்ரணவானந்தரும்) குரு சிஷ்யருக்கு உபதேசங்கள்	120
41.	ஸ்ரீ ஸஹஸ்ராக்ஷரீ வித்யா	2020 சாதுர்மாஸ்ய மலர்	84
42.	*Shakta Upanishats*	*Upanishats* about *Sri Devi*	385
43.	ஶாக்த உபநிஷதங்கள்	*Upanishats* about *Sri Devi*	400
44.	ஸ்ரீ **தேவீ கீதை**	Sri Devi Geeta	194
45.	*Śrī Devī Gīta*	Sri Devi Geeta	180
46.	*Śrī Gāyatrī Sahasranamam*	1,000 Divine Names of *Śrī Gāyatrī Mātā*	392
47.	ஸ்ரீ **காயத்ரீ** ஸஹஸ்ரநாமம்	ஸ்ரீ **காயத்ரி** மாதாவின் 1,000 திவ்ய நாமங்கள்	450
48.	ஸ்ரீ **ஸௌளந்தர்யலஹரீ**	ஒரு உள் அறிவு	250
49.	*Śrī Soundaryalaharī*	an Insight	200
		Applied Samskrutam Based	
50.	*Paribhāshā Stora–s*	An exploration of *Lalita Sahasranāmam*	96
51.	பரி**பாஷா** ஸ்தோத்ரங்கள்	ஸ்ரீ லலிதா ஸஹஸ்ரநாமம் ஒரு ஆய்வு	135
52.	*Shrī Cakra*, An Esoteric Approach	Mathematical Construction to draw *Shrī Cakra*	64
53.	ஸ்ரீ சக்கரம் வரையும் முறை	ஸ்ரீ சக்கரம் வரைய கணித கட்டுமானம்	84
54.	Number System in Samskrutam	An overview of Mathematics based on Samskrutam	123
55.	ஸமஸ்க்ருதத்தில் எண்ணியல்	ஸமஸ்க்ருதத்தில் பொதிந்துள்ள எண் கணிதம்	140
56.	*Vedic* Mathematics	30 formulae elucidated	146
57.	Vedic IT	Information Technology and Samskrutam	162
		IT Based	
58.	Orthogonal Array	A Statistical Tool for Software Testing	180
		Banking Based	
59.	Retail Banking	A guide book for Novice	213
60.	Corporate Banking	A guide book for Novice	232
61.	Dictionary of Financial Terms	A Guide Book for all – Demystifying Myriad Global Financial Terms	215
62.	GRC in BFS Industry	(**G**overnance, **R**isk Management and **C**ompliance by Banking & Finance Industry)	200

*****

Bibliography

The following books were referred to write this book. Lot many thanks to the authors and the publishers. They were very useful.

#	Title of the book	Author/ Publishers
1.	Soundaryalaharee	Tetiyoor Subrahmanya Sastrihal
2.	Sri Soundaryalaharee	Giri Publishing.
3.	Other books of the same author.	

*****

www.ingramcontent.com/pod-product-compliance
Lightning Source LLC
LaVergne TN
LVHW010017200726
843495LV00015B/1808